Children of the Changing South

T0055269

Children of the Changing South

*Accounts of Growing Up
During and After Integration*

Edited by FOSTER DICKSON

Afterword by David Molina

McFarland & Company, Inc., Publishers
Jefferson, North Carolina, and London

Reuben Jackson's poem "Sunday Brunch" reprinted with permission.

Stephanie Powell Watts' essay originally appeared as "Finding Black Power" in the *Oxford American*, Issue 64, March 2009.

LIBRARY OF CONGRESS CATALOGUING-IN-PUBLICATION DATA

Children of the changing South : accounts of growing up
  during and after integration / edited by Foster Dickson ;
  afterword by David Molina.
        p.   cm.
  Includes bibliographical references and index.

  ISBN 978-0-7864-6048-9
  softcover : 50# alkaline paper ∞

  1. Children — Southern States — Social conditions — 20th
century — Anecdotes.   2. Children — Southern States — Social
life and customs — 20th century — Anecdotes.   3. Children —
Southern States — Biography — Anecdotes.   4. Southern States —
Biography — Anecdotes.   5. Southern States — Race relations —
History — 20th century — Anecdotes.   6. Social change —
Southern States — History — 20th century — Anecdotes.
7. Southern States — Social conditions — 1945- — Anecdotes.
8. Southern States — Social life and customs — 20th century —
Anecdotes.   I. Dickson, Foster.
HQ792.U5C4335 2012
305.23097509'04 — dc23   2011038316

BRITISH LIBRARY CATALOGUING DATA ARE AVAILABLE

© 2012 Foster Dickson. All rights reserved

*No part of this book may be reproduced or transmitted in any form
or by any means, electronic or mechanical, including photocopying
or recording, or by any information storage and retrieval system,
without permission in writing from the publisher.*

On the cover: Participants in the civil rights march from Selma
to Montgomery, Alabama, in 1965 (Photograph by Peter Pettus)
Front cover design by Victoria Fenstermaker
(www.showcasedsign.com)

Manufactured in the United States of America

McFarland & Company, Inc., Publishers
  Box 611, Jefferson, North Carolina 28640
    www.mcfarlandpub.com

Table of Contents

Table of Contents

Preface

Children of the Changing South is a collection of memoirs by people who grew up in the southeastern United States in the mid-twentieth century, from the 1950s to the early 1990s. This sampling of narrative recollections, centered on Southern childhood during the turbulent times when changes were occurring, has been collected and is arranged to show the breadth and complexity of formative experiences of Southerners who are now modern-day adults. While much attention has been paid to the adults who led the efforts for change in the South, as well as to the adults who led the effort to stop the changes, less attention has been paid to this group of on-lookers, who were sometimes unwitting participants.

The critical and scholarly aims of putting together the collection work toward a more modern, multicultural view of Southern writing and literature (and history) that will transcend old-school dichotomous paradigms — for example, regarding white writers within a dominant tradition that leaves black writers within a secondary tradition, or regarding writers of traditional (or even stereotypical) Southern works in a dominant tradition that relegates newer Southern narratives to a secondary tradition. While the great Southern writers like Faulkner and Welty told important truths about the South of their day, the time has come for Southern writing to take its place fully in a new era. The South has evolved tremendously in the four decades since the time historians regard as the end of the Civil Rights Movement: the 1970s, 1980s, 1990s and 2000s. The old Southern traditions — both negative and positive ones — do still live on in various forms, but newer Southern experiences often wait to be told while the classics of Southern writing live on as undisputed champions of the Southern canon. The memoirs in this collection move on from the old South into the evolutionary period of the mid to late twentieth century.

The focus of *Children of the Changing South* has presented two major challenges with at least one major benefit. The first challenge has been the reticence and sometimes downright nastiness from some members of the

1

scholarly community who doubt a book of this subject can be viable and important. Because a great deal of scholarly attention is paid to the fiery and complex years of the Civil Rights Movement, which provides a gracious plenty of intriguing subjects, and to the complex post–World War II period and Great Depression years that led up to the movement, which evidence the shifting dynamics that empowered the movement, some people have expressed doubt to me that a book of memoirs that collects a sampling of Civil Rights-era or post–Civil Rights-era childhood provides anything important to public or scholarly discourse. Of course, if you are holding this book in your hands, then you are aware that I disagree. The ideas expressed in this collection reside in bringing together a roughly chronological series of narratives that begin in the late 1950s when Jim Crow was still fully entrenched and proceed forward through the 1960s, into 1970s when the movement proper was over, then further into the post-movement South of the 1980s and early 1990s. The collection contains the memoirs of both white and African-American writers, both men and women, with good geographic diversity, allowing for comparisons among settings, descriptions, and reactions, which tell a larger story of how people in the South have changed.

The second major challenge dealt with collecting the memoirs. For this collection, I put out a series of calls to writers to ask themselves the tough questions about having grown up in the changing South. For the first call, I received a healthy number of submissions with important themes and messages (but also some works that were inappropriate for this collection). The valid and useful answers I received were as diverse as the questions are difficult. In a factor for which I have no explanation, the vast majority of responses to the first call for submissions came from white women. Very few men responded at all and also very few African Americans. This fact prompted the later calls; for the collection to have any claim to importance, the voices had to be diverse. Later calls and the responses to those calls helped to make the collection more balanced.

One major benefit can arise from having this collection available for public and scholarly readings. Aside from the quality of the writing, which can provide enjoyable reading, the stories in *Children of the Changing South* provide glimpses into the life experiences of people who grew up in the South during the mid-and late twentieth century and who are today adults that are engaged in public discourse; they are the writers, teachers, scholars and historians who have made their life's work of conveying their ideas to others. As complex as the culture of the mid-century South may have been, modern Southern culture is complex as well. This collection provides a cross-section of reactions to some events and circumstances of the Civil Rights Movement and its aftermath, with an eye toward how the social changes affected the generations who would grow up to live in (and also lead) the latter-day South.

Introduction

by FOSTER DICKSON

> *Multiculturalists acknowledge the unbreakable linkage between stan-*
> *dards of aesthetic value and power: aesthetic judgments of any indi-*
> *vidual work are not made in a vacuum but are, rather, intimately*
> *connected with dominant cultural standards of value. And yet, every*
> *day critics and teachers of literature continue to assess, evaluate, judge*
> *and select literature. But here is the danger: Without new principles,*
> *many scholars and teachers tend to fall back on the familiar, and the*
> *cycle regenerates itself.*
> — Laurie Grobman, in *Multicultural Hybridity* (65)

As we begin the second decade of the twenty-first century, publications about the Civil Rights Movement in the South and its effects have flourished. Traditionally published books and articles, new online offerings, and accessibly archived documents by and about movement leaders easily number in the thousands. In addition to those works and documents, more stories have surfaced in recent decades, and now lesser-known figures have had and are having their say about the overall narrative of the Civil Rights Movement, which is still being compiled, organized and analyzed. However, though much attention has been paid to the adults who led, participated in or witnessed the Civil Rights Movement, much less attention has been paid to the people who were children during that time and during the period after the movement, when every conceivable notion of social protocol with respect to race had been threatened, discredited or dismantled, and when the adults who were their parents, teachers, aunts and uncles, neighbors, and friends were sifting through the wreckage of an old social order, the only way the South had ever known, trying to figure it out for themselves while trying to lead the little ones through the process of growing up.

These children of the South grew up and formed their most basic ideas about life during difficult times. Even though the South's major tectonic shift occurred in the area of race, this facet of Southern culture was not the only one that was shifting. The new social ideals from two different "waves" of the Women's Movement eventually trickled with time into the conservative South, too. (For example, trends in country music can be one barometer of mainstream Southern culture, and while singer Tammy Wynette may have been singing "Stand by Your Man" in 1968, another country singer Loretta Lynn was telling a different story of Southern womanhood a short while later in her 1975 song, "The Pill.") Yet, issues of race and gender roles were not the only factors that were changing. Modernization, a new kind of industrialism and a re-branding of the South as the "Sun Belt" produced new job opportunities, offered a new kind of economic mobility, and changed ideas about social class. At the same time that the old ideas about race then gender roles were being forced out, the South was also losing is predominantly rural lifestyle. All of those changes produced a Southern region unlike any seen before, and the effects were dramatic, including a slow political shift from the Democratic Party's "Solid South" to a reliable Republican stronghold. With drastic alterations to the fabric of society, the family, and politics occurring during the 1950s, 1960s and 1970s, with the dust only beginning to settle in the 1980s, the children of these decades were growing up amidst situations and statements they did not understand, and that even the adults in their lives may not have understood. For many of those children, the time has come to reflect on those formative years.

By viewing these events — and the memoirs contained in this collection — through the lens of multiculturalism, a critical movement with a post–Civil Rights roots, we can achieve some understanding of how the pre–Civil Rights Movement South evolved into the South of the late twentieth and early twenty-first centuries. Although multiculturalism is difficult to define — partially because the idea itself defies the concept of essentialism, partially because of open arguments among varying factions of critics who consider themselves multiculturalists — I use the concept loosely here to mean a social and critical view that values diversity, tolerance and equity over domination, intolerance and injustice.

The multiculturalism that I proffer here resembles what scholar Laurie Grobman has called "hybrid" multiculturalism, which attempts to reconcile "liberal multiculturalism" that tends to emphasize our commonality with "critical multiculturalism" that tends to emphasize a respectful recognition of difference. I believe that, in order to present the subject of this book adequately, both ideas must be present: recognition of what we share and recognition of what makes us different from each other. Finally, even though it is a compilation of literary works, *Children of the Changing South* encompasses a broader approach, as Theo David Goldberg writes in his "Preface" to his 1994 collection, *Multiculturalism: A Critical Reader*: "The debates around multiculturalism are also multi-and interdisciplinary. They necessarily involve politics and pedagogy, science and social science, the humanities and cultural studies, women's studies and ethnic studies, race, ethnicity, class, gender, nation, public administration, law, and political economy" (ix). To view the works in the collection only as literary works would be fiercely inadequate.

The Study of Children, as Narrators and Social Commentators

This collection, *Children of the Changing South*, is not the first work to use the platform of youth to discuss this historical period, but its contents are markedly different from previous works. Two of the more famous of youthful narratives from the time period covered in this collection are the nonfiction memoir *Selma, Lord, Selma*, written by journalist Frank Sikora from the words of Rachel West Nelson and Sheyann Webb-Christburg, who were both involved in Civil Rights Movement activities in Selma, Alabama in the mid–1960s, or the fiction novel *To Kill a Mockingbird* by Harper Lee, whose own life provided a rough basis for the events witnessed by Scout Finch in Maycomb, Alabama. Where these two works convey two overarching sets of truths about the mythic South of old, the memoirs collected in *Children of the Changing South* explore a diverse range of varying experiences that begin in the Jim Crow-era South and move forward into more modern times, in order to express that reducing the experience of a mid-century Southern childhood to a few easily manageable paradigms is not possible, while also providing compelling storytelling about Southern life. The complexity of having grown up during and right after the Civil Rights Movement in the South, for both black and white children, is staggering, and this collection provides a sampling of eighteen stories about that topic.

When I was young, in the 1970s and 1980s, I hadn't ever heard the terms "post-racial" or "feminist" and would not have known what they meant if I had. However, the South as it existed before I was born experienced immense changes that involved both of these ideas. In her now infamous chronicle, *Killers of the Dream*, which was published in 1961, Lillian Smith wrote about an older South, the South of *her* childhood, whose deep-seated contradictions resulted in a hypocritical scenario that was supported by the pillars of puritanical guilt, sexual repression, and a dictatorial patriarchy that allowed white men almost total freedom, while leaving white women and all African Americans with almost none. But growing up in a different South, during my childhood, after the Civil Rights Movement had ended, left me and many of us who were young then to navigate life that was a barrage of almost impossible daily dilemmas about living in an integrated, possibly post-racial society, and one in which women were not the conflicted and hopelessly powerless creatures that Lillian Smith described. Even if those of us who were young then did not know what we might have been asking, we are finding now, as adults, that we were pondering deeply troubling questions, even only in our minds. The South of Lillian Smith's youth rested its social order on these circumstances, and it is reported that her decline in popularity was a result of her statements in *Killers of the Dream*, which uncovered and described in detail what many Southerners had always known about their culture, but the South of my youth was a different animal, one that no one had ever actually seen, other than in their wildest dreams or worst nightmares. The South of my childhood — as I remember it — was far less burdened by the types of religious, political and social oppressiveness that Lillian Smith purports.

The children of the Civil Rights and post–Civil Rights eras, some of whose memoirs are included in this volume, had only the notions about race that we got from our parents, but often had no solid notions of the power struggles involved with social class or gender, while all of the dramas were being played out on little stages all around us all of the time. For the children of the 1950s through the 1980s, the confusion was very real, as we looked to our elders for the guidance that they were mostly incapable of providing. Maybe we noticed that another kid didn't look we did, but it didn't matter much. Maybe we noticed that some other kid's house was bigger or smaller than our own, or that they had more toys than us, or that their bike was better than ours. Maybe we noticed that our mothers did the dishes almost all the time, while our fathers lounged around after dinner. But we certainly did not understand the social issues associated racism, sexism and classism. With the passing of youth and the coming adulthood, that would change.

As children of these times grew older, we who were raised between the 1950s and 1980s began to pay attention to the reality around us, and in some cases we were even forced to pay attention by the pronouncements and diatribes of our confused or dismayed parents. In addition to the normal struggles of growing up, these generations faced the decades of the

1960s, 1970s and 1980s, which brought massive changes to the culture of the South, as racial integration became the status quo (at least officially and superficially), and as the divorce rate skyrocketed, and the hard questions about this new America received everyone's attention.

In recent years, attention of writers and scholars is being paid to the youthful, formative experiences of these generations. In October 1995, The University of Mississippi — "Ole Miss" as it is affectionately known — held its annual three-day Porter L. Fortune Jr. History Symposium, which that year focused on "Childhood in the South," and hosted discussions of topics ranging from children in slavery to Robert Moses' Algebra Project. The symposium's online description of the 1995 event asked and answered,

> Why study the history of childhood in the South? One reason is simply that children make up too large a segment of the population for historians to ignore them. But considering the issue of childhood should also shed new light on many crucial issues in the study of the South.

The symposium, which is named for the former university chancellor who served during the post-integration period from 1968 to 1984, was "sponsored by the History Department, the Afro-American Studies Program, and the Center for the Study of Southern Culture, receives funding from the Mississippi Humanities Council."

Additionally, in relatively recent years, some public and scholarly attention has been directed toward works that involving Southern tales of childhood and growing up. In the modern American mainstream, two prominent Southern narratives stand out. Of course, after its 1960 Pulitzer Prize and the film's subsequent Academy Awards in 1963, *To Kill A Mockingbird* is continually read, studied and lauded as one of the best American stories ever told. Additionally, after its 1997 release as a book, *Selma, Lord, Selma* was release as an acclaimed film in 1999. Within the scholarly community, other more specific subjects have also been addressed. At the risk of cataloguing articles *ad nausem*, two examples follow. Post-dating the 1994 re-release of Lillian Smith's *Killers of the Dream*, *The American Quarterly* published Jay Watson's "Uncovering the Body, Discovering Ideology: Segregation and Sexual Anxiety in Lillian Smith's *Killers of the Dream*," in September 1997. More recently, Holly Virginia Blackford's "Uncle Tom Melodrama with a Point of View: *To Kill a Mockingbird*" appeared in the recent book, *Telling Children's Stories: Children's Literature and Narrative Theory*, which is a collection of scholarly works on children's literature subjects, though not all Southern.

As a more recent book-length example of real interest being shown in Southern childhood, *Children of the Movement* by features writer John Blake of the *Atlanta Journal-Constitution* was published in 2004, albeit with the bulky subtitle: *The sons and daughters of Martin Luther King, Jr., Malcolm X, Elijah Muhammad, George Wallace, Andrew Young, Julian Bond, Stokely Carmichael, Bob Moses, James Chaney, Elaine Brown, and others reveal how the civil rights movement tested and transformed their families.* Blake interviewed and wrote about the now-grown children of famed movement-era figures from both sides of the struggle. In his introduction, Blake posits some of his reasons for seeking out and exploring his subjects, as well as providing some hints at what he discovered along the way, and he ends that short section by writing:

> As we move forward through a new century, the movement is in danger of being obscured by sentimentality. [...] The movement's aftershocks continue to ripple through the lives of its veterans and their children — just as its political implications continue to ignite freedom struggles around the world. What happened back then shapes all our lives today — even those of us who dismiss that era.
> In a sense, we are all children of the movement [xi–xii].

He touches on two important points that are juxtaposed, even though in his words, they may not seem to be. Southerners — and possibly all Americans — are indeed all "children of the movement," because it "shapes all our lives today." There is almost no way for modern-day Southerners to escape completely from the aftermath of the Civil Rights Movement, and the children who grew up in its heyday or in its wake were affected deeply.

Changes in Racial Attitudes: Toward a Multicultural South

At the risk of oversimplifying very complex history, a general description of the changes in Southern race relations is necessary here, with a focus on the subject matter within *Children of the Changing South*. The climate of race relations changed dramatically and quickly (in historical terms) during the period of this book's focus. The earliest time setting for a narrative in this collection is 1958, and the latest childhood memories that are discussed occur in the early 1990s. In 1957, the South was still in an uproar over the possible implications of *Brown v. Board of Education*, yet by that time the Montgomery Bus Boycott had been successful; its victory in a 1956 US Supreme Court decision set the movement fully in motion. However, in 1958, the tempestuous events at Central High School in Little Rock, Arkansas, when the National Guard would usher the black students later dubbed the "Little Rock Nine" into school, were current events. The racial climate of the first memoir in this collection, "Power, Love and a Sound Mind" by Jacqueline Wheelock, is very different from the later memoirs; and, because the work contains a juxtaposition of Wheelock's own child memories of the late 1950s with her experiences as a teacher in the 1970s, the earlier parts of this one work even lie in stark contrast to its latter parts.

By the time of the second memoir in this collection, set in 1964, the Civil Rights Movement was in full swing, and changes in laws that allowed for racial segregation and discrimination were toppling like dominoes. The sit-ins of 1960 and the Freedom Rides of 1961 stand out as major successes for the platform of change, while the Albany Movement of 1961–1962 stands out as a defeat. The momentum continued as the early years of the 1960s saw the efforts of James Meredith in Mississippi and of the Children's March in Alabama, while the negative side-effects of the movement were manifest in the violence that led Birmingham being dubbed "Bombingham" and in the murder of Medgar Evers. By 1964, the time frame of the second memoir in this collection, President Lyndon Johnson was signing the Civil Rights Act, and the state of Mississippi would add the term "Freedom Summer" and the names of Goodman, Schwerner and Chaney to America's lexicon. The racial climate of Lean'tin Bracks' school years, and the fear of violence associated with the period, is indicative of the mid–1960s, and distinctive and unique in the collection.

By the late 1960s, which serves as the time setting for three subsequent pieces in the collection, the new path for racial integration was set for the children growing up during this time period. The many local challenges to the slow, evasive maneuvering of school systems avoiding integration were dismantling racially segregated education all over the South; the presence of diversity in classrooms was becoming a reality. Public facilities and privately owned businesses alike were becoming fully integrated by the late 1960s, yet the rise of a new class of black elected officials had not yet occurred. Regarding a more personal aspect of Southerners' lives, in 1967 the US Supreme Court ruled unanimously in *Loving v. Virginia* that miscegenation laws, which forbade interracial marriages, were unconstitutional. In the next year, Martin Luther King, Jr., was shot and killed in 1968, and hopes for a post–Civil Rights focus on universal poverty rights diminished with his death. Though history would later tell us that the most prominent examples of violence were done by the 1960s' end, the period was not without tension, as evidenced in the memoirs of integrated-school experiences Jim Grimsley, Lillie Anne Brown, and Becky McLaughlin, who each had his or her own run-in with those tensions.

The 1970s ushered in a different kind of Southern life with respect to race. Most scholars mark the end of the Civil Rights Movement in the late 1960s, mostly commonly with the death of Martin Luther King, Jr. By the end of the 1960s, Southern states were seeing the first African Americans since Reconstruction to be elected to major state offices, like Douglas Wilder in Virginia. Even though these changes went beyond the South — as exemplified by the election of leaders like New York's Shirley Chisholm and the expansion of the Black Panther Party into nationwide political force — the Southern culture did its daily business under the microscope of government and national media attention. This climate provides the backdrop for the memoirs by Leslie Haynsworth and Georgene Bess Montgomery, who both describe navigating the new terrain, as well as some of the backdrop for the memoir by Glenis Redmond, which weaves backward and forward in time from her youth in the late 1960s and 1970s to her later experiences as an adult. Jacqueline Wheelock's latter-day portions land her experiences as an adult in the 1970s, as well.

By the late 1970s and into the 1980s, new patterns of racial interaction were more developed. Racial integration within day-to-day life was prevalent, although social equality had not been achieved. Within this new social structure, the presence of hard-dying old habits, the storytelling and reminiscing about the past by older generations, and the constant confusion about etiquette and propriety created a tense and cursory politeness that often masked underlying fears and anxieties. Eight memoirs in this collection, by Stephanie Powell Watts, Camika Spencer, Ashley Day, Anne Estepp, Dawne Shand, Ravi Howard, Lynn Watson, and Kyes Stevens, deal with this period of time. Each writer tells a different story, from Watts' recollections of her parents discussing the loss of their all-black school to Watson's conclusions that social class was allotted far more importance than race, or from Spencer's discussions of the differences between the white suburban school and the black urban school to Stevens' examinations of the differences in what constituted poverty and what roles communities play in helping anyone regardless of race. The complexity of reactions among both white and black families left far more questions than answers, questions that these younger generations would have face.

As more modern times approach, the early 1990s showed real change and the beginnings of an acceptance of a multicultural South, while the legacy of the old South still did lurk — as Margaret Rose Gladney noted in the aforementioned introduction to the 1994 edition of *Killers of the Dream*—both at home in the South and through the nation as a whole. Although children may not have been taught about how different the South of the late 1980s and 1990s was from the South before the 1970s, the facts of that old South still lingered. The political climate had changed so drastically in the decades since the most difficult years of the movement. Although Alabama governor George Wallace proclaimed in his 1963 inauguration speech that he would ensure "segregation now, segregation tomorrow, segregation forever," he had publicly apologized for those actions by the late 1970s; by the 1990s, President Bill Clinton, who had been governor of another Southern state, Arkansas, was "apologizing for slavery." (As a more modern note on the ongoing changes in the area, in 2009, the US Senate would pass its bill that served as an official apology for "slavery and Jim Crow.") The two final memoirs in *Children of the Changing South*, by Ray Morton and Kathleen Rooney, are set firmly in this latter-day Southern culture. Their works show a changed and somewhat confused consciousness of race and a consciousness of the South and its history as symbols.

While changes in the area of race cast the longest shadows on modern Southern history, other significant factors are important as well. As a multicultural South emerged, one where new voices were to be heard, more new voices than only those of African-American men were gaining strength. After all, many local struggles within the larger Civil Rights Movement were pushed forward by women.

Changes in the Lives of Women ... and Families

We now know that the preoccupation over the racial issues of the period often obscures or diverts attention to other issues of change in the South, including matters of women's rights. The South has never been known as a place friendly to women's rights. As an early example, Southern states, with the exception of Tennessee, were exceptionally slow to ratify the 19th Amendment to the US Constitution, which provided for women's right to vote. Even though the Amendment became federal law after enough states had ratified it, the South lagged far behind in its formal acceptance. As examples, after failed ratification votes in 1919 and 1920, Virginia ratified the 19th Amendment in 1952, Alabama in 1953, Florida and South Carolina in 1969, Georgia and Louisiana in 1970, North Carolina in 1971 ... and Mississippi in 1984!

Although the mainstream acceptance of "feminism" in the South is still precarious in a region that is notoriously conservative, certain national trends and events affected Southern women, even if it has been more slowly. In the 1960s, the birth control pill became widely available; Betty Friedan's *Feminine Mystique* was published; the National Organization for Women (NOW) was founded, among other significant events that are sometimes dubbed the "Second Wave" of the Women's Rights movement. However, as an example of slower change in the South, Louisiana's first woman to be a state senator, Virginia Kilpatrick Shehee, was elected in 1975.

Numan Bartley writes, in *The New South, 1945–1980*, about the Southern hesitation toward granting equality to women. He notes that the Civil Rights Act of 1964 did not originally include anti-discrimination protection on the basis of gender, but that it was added. Additionally, Bartley writes that Southern states were as slow to respond to the 1972 Equal Rights Amendment as they had been to the 19th Amendment fifty-five years earlier:

> The legislatures in Texas and Tennessee ratified the Equal Rights Amendment by large majorities in the spring of 1972, and soon afterward the Kentucky legislature approved it by a close vote in both houses. Thereafter, the amendment's success in the South ended. In 1974 Tennessee rescinded ratification, and in 1978 the Kentucky legislature voted to rescind ratification and Governor Julian Carroll vetoed the rescinder. Texas turned out to be the only southern state to endorse the amendment unequivocally. In the end, the states rejected the Equal Rights Amendment, and ten of the fifteen states that never ratified it were southern [426].

Despite this lack of support for the ideals of equality for women, Bartley acknowledges that this change occurred nonetheless in recognizable ways, for example: "More women entered the workforce: in 1970 women made up 39 percent of it, and in 1980 they amounted to 43 percent" (428).

Another issue in the South, as in the nation as a whole, was the sky-rocketing divorce rate during the period covered in *Children of the Changing South*. According to one study, "[d]ivorce increased almost 40 percent from 1970 to 1975,"* and in this factor, the South was no exception. According to some speculations, divorce rates in the South are higher than national averages because Southerners tend to get married younger, which leads to conflicts as the partners mature. As the wives of Southern men grew up from the young, often submissive brides that they once were, and moreover grew up amidst the well-publicized provocations of feminism, they have

*http://www.divorcereform.org/rates.html#anchor1223885

in large numbers left those marriages that were full of limitations, and have almost always taken the children with them. Two US Census tables from the "Household and Family Characteristics: March 1978" report provide a basic overview of this trend on the national level; in the first chart, titled "Composition of Households, 1960 to 1978," the "Married Couple with Children" category dropped from 44.1 percent to 32.4 percent and the "One Parent with Children" category rose from 4.4 percent to 7.3 percent, while in another chart titled "Characteristics of Families Maintained by Women: 1960 to 1978," the "Divorced" category under "Marital Status," more than doubled from 15.9 percent in 1960 to 33.8 percent in 1978. (No state-by-state data is available in the report.)

The changes in women's lives and the make-up of families brought on by these changes, accompanying the already prevalent changes in the area of race, affected the South and its children dramatically as well. In Leslie Haynsworth's "Working Women and Women Working" and in Kyes Stevens' "Attempts to Bury History Backfire," readers will find narratives of the direct impact on women and families in an emergent multicultural South, including in areas of economic opportunity, educational opportunities, and the definition of social classes within a larger framework where a person's race and gender held significant meanings. Leslie Haynsworth makes a direct assessment of the how the lives of women were affected by new opportunities, including who got to take advantage of those opportunities and who did not, especially with respect to race. Kyes Stevens also remarks directly how women's lives were affected, especially in areas of domestic work, and especially in the nuanced ways that factors of race and social class intersect with traditional gender roles. As an emergent new South was taking root, and as the nation focused much attention on expanding notions of justice and equality with respect to race, changes in the lives of women must not be ignored.

Changes in Lifestyle, Economic Opportunity and Social Structure

While historic changes were occurring in the South in the areas of race relations and women's roles in society, concepts of socio-economic status and social class were also changing for reasons related to industrialization and modernization. As one main example, urbanization was changing the lives of Southerners as they moved away from rural, farming lifestyles. In his 1987 book, *Rural Worlds Lost: The American South, 1920–*

1960, historian Jack Temple Kirby describes the scenario — as it leads up to the time period covered in *Children of the Changing South*— in his fourth chapter, "Folks, Communities and Economies in Flux":

> Change — a term used synonymously in western culture with progress and modernization — occurs every moment. People usually become aware of deep changes only after the working out of many structural processes, and once it is recognized, change seems to have occurred suddenly. Modernization tran-spired this way. Its impact was most intense during the 1930s and 1940s in most parts of the South, but modernization began long before and it contin-ues still. The phenomenon manifested itself in a variety of stages at various times over sub-regions of the South. The cash nexus, machines, paved roads, and supermarkets appeared earliest in the most physically accessible places, later in the most remote [118].

This description sums up what Kirby spends the bulk of his book elabo-rating: that the South is like any other place in America, because it enjoyed a mid-century period of industrial modernization, which led to urbaniza-tion. At the end of that same chapter, Kirby states, "Modernization wrought the most severe changes for those millions of plantation-belt land-less, for highlanders, and for white-land southerners, both black and white. For them there was no life-sustaining place left on the land. Many had no choice but migration" (154).

For the South of the Great Depression and World War II eras, this socio-economic paradigm shift — along with other factors — created the circumstances that made the social equality movements of mid-century possible. For instance, most historians agree that the presence of unions in the African-American community provided the basis for structural plan-ning in the later Civil Rights Movement. By mid-century, a newly neces-sitated geographic mobility caused a new kind of social mobility, unlike the old caste system of plantation culture. Also, with people now being more concentrated in cities, organizing and educating lower-income and middle-class people become easier and more feasible.

The children of the post-war South grew up under entirely different circumstances than their parents and grandparents who had come of age during the rural times of the Great Depression. Even after the post-war period had ended, the changes grew even more drastic; according to Kirby, "[i]n 1959, there were 508,061 small farms in the South," but "[b]y 1969 their numbers had shrunk by 39 percent to 307,697" (347). Jack Temple Kirby ends his book, literally, with the following statement: "A new New South had appeared, but whether it was better than the old one was a ques-tion not easily and fairly answered" (360). The changes would continue.

These urbanizing and modernizing trends affected the lives of the children growing up during this period. As populations became more centralized, educational opportunities become more logistically possible. New technologies in modernized households, including the television, allowed for a world view that differed from the isolated perspective of a rural, farming life. The increased prevalence of automobiles, and later two-car households, improved mobility for the whole family. However these changes may have improved the condition of day-to-day life, they did not add up to equally better lives for all Southerners.

With respect to social class, one obvious development, in the area of schools and education, showed white Southerners in particular who stood where. The highly unofficial "academy system" developed all over the South in the wake of school integration, as the more affluent white parents created small private schools for the families that could afford it, leaving the children of poorer white families to remain in the integrated public schools that all of them had dreaded. After decades of calls for white unity against black insurrections, the white families of lower socio-economic classes found themselves abandoned to deal in a direct way to the day-to-day realities of the new order. Look at the founding dates of many established private schools in the South, and you will see dates that range from the mid–1950s, when the *Brown v. Board of Education* lawsuit was won, into the 1970s, when the last of the holdout school systems were giving up on political maneuvering and accepting defeat in their prolonged fights against integration.

As a middle-class lifestyle became more available to more people, new socio-economic patterns were commingled with post–Civil Rights social changes with respect to race. The children who grew up among these new scenarios were often severed from the South that their parents knew, which was often a low-income, isolated, racially segregated, rural life in which localized power was concentrated into a few wealthy hands. However, in this newer, more urbanized, more mobile South, the commingling of unlike elements not only became possible, but very real.

Changes in the Political Landscape: The "Reddening" of the South

In addition to the mid-century changes and the South's shifts toward a more participatory and multicultural environment in the areas of race, the roles of women, and social class were not significant enough, the political changes make up another dimension to the already confusing scene. The children of this period grew up during a time when the cultural climate of the South provided no solid precedent for an understanding of the American political landscape; while this is negligible with respect to small children, it is more important to teenagers who were forming many kinds of opinions about the world. Southerners of the early 1960s witnessed a Democratic Party that encompassed both John F. Kennedy and George Wallace. Yet, one fact held true: the South's conservative ideals would win out over its party loyalty, with a slow, decades-long shift from mid-century Democratic dominance to Republican dominance by the early twenty-first century. Although politics is an aspect of life that affects adults far more than it does children, to neglect it in this discussion would be a mistake.

Despite an at least surface-level acceptance of the post–Jim Crow social and political landscape, the South had and continues to have a notoriously conservative streak that shows itself often enough. One truth about the South's response to the changes in American society since the 1960s is called the "reddening of the South." Once solidly Democratic, the Southern states today lean heavily Republican, with the "wave" of Republican popularity in the 2010 mid-term elections representing the last straw for many Democratic strongholds.

However, even though the shifts were more defined and recognizable by the 1960s, they had begun earlier. In his 2004 book, *Before Brown: Civil Rights and White Backlash in the Modern South*, editor and business professor Glenn Feldman compiled nine scholarly essays that examine Civil Rights Movement activities and the Southern white responses to those actions during the 1930s and 1940s. Even though his work's focus is the pre-movement era (and this collection involves the movement and post-movement eras), Feldman's "Epilogue," which is subtitled "Race, Emotion and the Rise of the Republican Party in Alabama and the South," focuses squarely on modern results. After commenting on the almost-total Democratic dominance of the South from the end of Reconstruction until the post–World War II Truman administration, Feldman writes about the political landscape post–New Deal, post–*Brown v. Board*, post–Rosa Parks.

> Once it became clear that the racial liberalism of FDR and Harry Truman would be continued by the national Democratic Party, huge numbers of conservative southern whites reconciled themselves to leaving the party for good. [...] As he signed the 1964 Civil Rights Bill into law, Lyndon Johnson [...] clearly understood this. No sooner had he signed the act than he slumped forward, took his head in his hands, and told his press secretary, "I've just given the South to the Republicans for a generation" [283].

Feldman goes on to write about Richard Nixon's "Southern Strategy," which exploited those divisions and helped him win the White House in 1968 and 1972, even though a popular Southerner who was quite good at exploiting racial divisions, George C. Wallace, was running against him. Another historian, William D. Barnard, also wrote in his 1974 book, *Dixiecrats and Democrats: Alabama Politics, 1942–1950*, about the earlier dissatisfaction with FDR and Truman and about the political shifting that had begun before the Civil Rights Movement began, specifically with the Dixiecrats or States' Rights Party (97).

During that forty-year period from 1960 to 2000, although Democrats continued to hold significant power on local and state levels, the Southern support of Republican presidential candidates far outweighed support of Democratic candidates. Only a Democratic presidential candidate from Arkansas with a running mate from Tennessee — Bill Clinton and Al Gore in 1992 — could even partially break the new hold the Republican Party had on the South's presidential voting practices since helping to elect Ronald Reagan. The victorious Clinton-Gore ticket carried five Southern states (Louisiana, Arkansas, Georgia, Kentucky and Tennessee), while the losing Republican Bush-Quayle ticket carried six Southern states (Mississippi, Alabama, Florida, North Carolina, South Carolina and Virginia). Before Clinton's successful first campaign, Georgia native and incumbent president Jimmy Carter only won his home state during his bid for a second term in 1980, while Reagan, a Californian, carried every other Southern state. (As the "reddening" has become almost complete, George H. W. Bush carried every Southern state in 1988, as did his son George W. Bush in 2000 and 2004. Most recently, Republication candidate John McCain carried ten of the twelve Southern states in his 2008 defeat to Barack Obama. As one example of the completion of state level "reddening," in Alabama, the 2010 elections brought a Republican majority to both houses of the state legislature for the first time in 136 years.)

The South's conservative streak is a well-documented and often-discussed aspect of the post–Civil Rights era South. In their 1975 book *Southern Politics & the Second Reconstruction*, Numan V. Bartley and Hugh D. Graham examine the details of Southern politics in the spirit of V.O. Key's 1949 opus, *Southern Politics: In State and Nation*. Their fourth chapter, "The Emergence of Two-Party Politics," describes the extent of Democratic dominance prior to 1960:

> In the five Deep South states, Republican gubernatorial and senatorial candidates rarely carried as much as one-fifth of the vote until the early 1960s. In Georgia, Mississippi and South Carolina, there were no Republican nominees

for governor until 1966; there was no serious nominee for senator until 1966 and in Georgia none at all until 1968. The only minor exceptions to this rule of Republican invisibility in the Deep South were in Alabama and Louisiana [82].

Later, in their sixth chapter, titled "The Ambiguous Resurgence of the New South," the authors write about the political shifts and the divergent attitudes of blue-collar whites, white-collar whites, and blacks regarding issues ranging from the candidates in the 1968 presidential election — Humphrey, Nixon and Wallace — to the differing opinions on the need for federal intervention for school integration or the right to open housing for blacks. Not surprisingly, upper-income and professional whites — the most conservative group — led the way to the Republican Party, with working-class whites coming to the GOP more slowly and African Americans mostly remaining politically Democratic.

In a later work of an entirely different tone and spirit, 1996's *Dixie Rising: How the South Is Shaping American Values, Politics and Culture*, Peter Applebome provides a stark yet startling description of the post–Civil Rights era South:

> Think of a place that's bitterly anti-government and fiercely individualistic, where race is a constant subtext to daily life, and God and guns run through public discourse like an electric current. Think of a place where influential scholars market theories of white supremacy, where the word "liberal" is a negative epithet, where hang-'em-high law-and-order justice centered on the death penalty and throw-away-the-key sentencing are politically all but unstoppable. Think of a place obsessed with states' rights, as if it were the 1850s all over again and the Civil War had never been fought [8].

Applebome's book, now about fifteen years old, was published in the midst of the Republican ascension in the South, at a time when a Georgia representative named Newt Gingrich was kicking off his "Contract with America."

Finally, as time went by, readings about the changes in the South's political leaning could be analyzed from a greater distance, as statistics and documents were compiled and made public. In a 2008 book titled *Wrong on Race: The Democratic Party's Buried Past*, writer and political adviser Bruce Bartlett describes what he calls "The Southern Strategy Myth" in his chapter, "Since the Civil Rights Act." He writes,

> The myth of Nixon's Southern strategy has been maintained for so many years because casual observation sees a shift in Southern voting patterns in the 1960s in which the historical dominance of the Democratic Party in that region began to break down. By the 1980s, the South was solidly Republican

in presidential races, with Republicans becoming very competitive in statewide races. By the 1990s, Republicans had become dominant across the board [171–172].

Bartlett goes on to explain in short order that too many people have assumed that race was the motivating factor behind the Southern vote shifting to the Republican Party, which has caused many of those same people to infer that Southerners found their new racist ally in the GOP; his assertion is that improved economic conditions, like a rising per capita income, actually led the move because conservative Southerners preferred the Republican platform of "low taxes and small government" (172). He is also quick to note that race may have been a factor in the change and that Nixon was, in fact, elected in 1968 over Wallace, thus "without the support of Southern racists" (173).

This fourth major change — adding the element of politics to the already staggering changes in racial mores, gender roles and socio-economic conditions — regardless of its reasoning, adds one more dimension to the confusion under which the younger generations would grow up. The rationale of individual Southerners can be questioned, but the "reddening" of the South cannot. Problematically, as the South has become more diverse in multiple ways, the region may have accomplished little more than trade a Democratic-based one-party politics for a Republican-based one-party system, yet through the latter decades of the twentieth century, there may have been real and viable political options.

A Multiculturalist's View of Southern Literature and History

In 1941, before any of the contributors in the volume were born, another attempt by a Southern writer, Wilbur J. Cash, to explain and assess the South that confused him was published: *The Mind of the South*. Cash was already dead from suicide by the time his now-infamous work saw its first sale, but the way he ended his book figures into what I am describing, the scenario into which the writers in this volume were born and raised. In his final chapter, "Of the Great Blight — and New Quandaries," Cash writes of formerly agricultural Southerners becoming urbanized and moving into cities and towns to work in mills, the circumstances of which caused an urge to look backward into what seemed like (supposedly) better times. Further, he wrote of the fears that unions — the organizing of economically depressed people — struck in rural landowners: "For if the unionism and the strikes succeeded in industry, would they not in time be likely to reach out into the countryside?" (347) And in his own poetic style, Cash even wonders aloud what might have been if the New Deal had succeeded in bringing about real change:

> Looking at the South in those days, indeed, one might readily have con-cluded that at last the old pattern was on its way to a conclusive break-up, that new ideas and a new tolerance were sweeping the field, and that the region as a whole, growing genuinely social-minded and realistic, was setting itself up to examine its problems with clear eyes and dispassionate temper — in a word, that the old long lag between the Southern mind and the changing conditions of the Southern world was about to end [368].

Cash goes on to do several more things: to mention that schools and other efforts at education seemed to be improving after the Depression had loos-ened its grip on the South; to extol progressive-minded thinkers like the "immediately valuable" Howard Odum at the University of North Car-olina; to discuss newer Southern writers of both the forward-looking and backward-looking varieties; and to explore the ideas of the literary South-ern Agrarians, all as examples of the multiple viewpoints about post–Depression Southern life. Even at the end of the Great Depression, Cash recognized that the Southern social and historical narrative was no longer being dominated by one point-of-view.

Two passages in the final pages of *The Mind of the South* lead my dis-cussion into a more modern context. First, in his next-to-last section of the book, Cash writes, "In large part, efforts to call attention to the prob-lems which exist have been treated not only as an unnecessary attempt at trouble-making but as a gross affront to the section" (424). Second, the book's final paragraph begins: "In the coming days and probably soon, it is likely to have to prove its capacity for adjustment far beyond what has been true in the past" (429). The memoirs in *Children of the Changing South* are evidence of that "capacity for adjustment" by showing a sampling of the forms that "adjustment" took. Literary works are not produced in a vacuum — they have definite social and historical contexts — and the underpinnings of these memoirs are definite and powerful.

W. J. Cash's prophetic ending about a "capacity for change" in *The Mind of the South* paves the way for an understanding of other develop-ments that led to the environment in this collection of memoirs from (reluctantly) multicultural South of mid-to late twentieth century. The seeds of the social turbulence had been planted already, during the 1930s and 1940s, when labor leaders had made efforts at organizing white and black workers alike. After the unease brought on by unionism, communism and other experiments in social equality, more changes followed. President Franklin D. Roosevelt's Executive Order 8802, issued in June 1941, created the Fair Employment Practices Commission (FEPC), which declared that discrimination in hiring for work that involved any government contract for the war effort was strictly prohibited; much of that work was done in the South. Also during World War II, women had gone to work while men were away at war, which gave them a new sense of independence and confidence. After the war was over, Harry Truman's Executive Order 9981, in July 1948, called for the desegregation of the US military. Early and immediate consequences of these types of changes included the ossification of Jim Crow and multiple attempts by state legislators and governors to entrench a systemic perpetuation of segregation. However, a small taste of equality had a bitter residue for many Southerners ... who were not white men. Efforts to stymie a multicultural South were numerous and prevalent.

Unfortunately for Southern demagogues, the political machinery that had helped them to maintain their systemic stranglehold on subjugated groups of people crumbled, then the Civil Rights Movement began in the wake of further changes. The 1954 *Brown v. Board of Education* decision negated the 1896 ruling *Plessy v. Ferguson* that had allowed "separate but equal" schools. Integration was beginning to occur in the workplace and in the military, but then it was becoming a reality in the schools, too. Racial tensions in the South were so high that massive conflict inevitably followed in the 1950s and 1960s. One prominent response to the possibility of a multicultural South was the "Southern Manifesto" of 1956 whose original draft was written by sensational segregationist US Senator Strom Thurmond of South Carolina.

Understanding that cohesive element of change (and resistance to it) within the context of the literary works in *Children of the Changing South* leads to another aspect of the total situation, which regards Southern history and historians. Because the middle to late twentieth century was a period of immense change in the South, the stories that have emerged (and that have been allowed to emerge) continue to make the South a different place, ever evolving. As the reexamination of the Civil Rights and post–Civil Rights years continues, some well-known authors and their classics of Southern studies have come back to assist, adding some updated points-of-view.

In 2002, Paul Gaston's *New South Creed: A Study in Southern Mythmaking*, originally published in 1970, was reissued with a new foreword and an "Afterword to the New Edition: Looking Backward, 2001–1970," which provides the author's ideas about the three decades after his book was originally published. In that afterword, Gaston writes:

> The story of the last third of the twentieth century differs from the last third of the nineteenth [century] in many ways, both in complexity and in fading regional differences, yet the Southern-born myth of the earlier period, instead of dissipating along with diminishing Southern distinctiveness and rising material status, found itself merging seamlessly with the national myths of innocence, prosperity, reconciliation, and triumph. In its new configuration it proved to be more influential than ever before [246].

Gaston acknowledges that the "myth" of the "New South," a long-standing idea that the South was voluntarily mending it racist and elitist ways, took a totality different shape in the post–Civil Rights era. This time, according to Gaston, the idea of a real "New South" *seemed* to suggest, as one tenet, that America would finally be healed and that the South would truly join the *United* States of America.

Somewhat earlier than Gaston's re-issued book, Lillian Smith's 1961 book *Killers of the Dream* was reissued again with a new introduction in 1994. Smith's book, which I have discussed a little bit already, deals with issues of childhood and how heavily the burdens of childhood confusion carry over into adulthood. The new introduction, written by American studies professor and social justice advocate Margaret Rose Gladney, states, "At the end of the twentieth century, Smith's words remain all too timely: today's children everywhere know the world is in trouble." The South may no longer be mired in what Gladney describes as "the physical and psychic destruction of the racist society in which they lived," but new challenges have faced the children who came after Smith, and Gladney clearly recognized that.

Children of the Changing South groups together a body of memoirs that span decades and even generations, in order to present a multicultural cross-section of literary works that are set in within a Southern historical context and examine Southern historical subjects, but which are not intended as works for the discipline of Southern history. The writers and works in this collection represent mostly new kinds of voices in the overall schema of Southern studies. In my experience, one factor that has most often caused voices to be turned away from the discourse in critical reflections on Southern culture is not race or gender or social class or political convictions, but age. Younger generations and the ideas of younger people are regularly excluded from the discourse, because of an overarching idea that, since younger people did not experience the Depression or the Civil

Rights Movement, we somehow missed the key element in what it means to be Southern. Scholars and critics of Southern culture have given time and attention to white and black perspectives, to men's and women's perspectives, to the perspectives of middle-class, working-class and lower-income groups, and to progressive and conservative perspectives. Lending credence to those diverse points-of-view is important, yet the discourse is ongoing and the perspectives of younger people, including those with post–Civil Rights perspectives, is necessary in this new South.

Recent attention has been paid to not only the movement years, but also the years that followed, in some in new books, too. These new works of Southern history have contributed to a multicultural view of these turbulent and subsequent recent decades in the South. Multicultural ideals seek to eliminate dichotomous models where only two opposing sides are present and where one dominates the other, in favor of a cooperative model of discourse that values all voices equally. Despite the fact that white Southerners long dominated African-American Southerners in political, economic and social contexts, control of the narrative of the Civil Rights Movement period has been dominated by the African-American perspective, largely because the white perspective often contained such regressive and offensive ideas. Where so much political, critical and scholarly attention has been paid to African-American narratives and perspectives, two relatively recent books, which also defy the "sentimentality" that John Blake lamented, have taken on subjects involving non-stereotypical perspectives on white Southerners.

First, in the 2006 book, *There Goes My Everything: White Southerners in the Age of Civil Rights, 1945–1975*, historian Jason Sokol explores the changing South through a plethora of reactions, both hostile and accommodating, of white Southerners to the race-based social upheaval from end of the World War II to the year before Jimmy Carter was elected. These books show a spark of interest in the most complex dynamics of Southern life and culture, as more than the dichotomous paradigm of "Southern Way of Life" vs. Martin Luther King, Jr., and King wins. *There Goes My Everything* does an excellent job of providing a more rounded view of Southern whites and of describing their fear, anxiety, and dismay during the post–Civil Rights years. For example, Sokol writes in the chapter, "'Softly, the Unthinkable': The Contours of Political and Economic Change," that "[i]n this world of upheaval, whites did not know precisely how to react," but he also acknowledges both the positive and negative sides of the situation:

New ways of seeing were evident in white citizens who had their attitudes transformed by the scenes of black protest, white cheerleaders who began to shuffle and sway alongside black girls, white proprietors who saw that the onset of integration did not cripple their businesses, and white politicians who discovered a language above and beyond racism. Of course, there were many stories to the contrary — of white politicians who simply packaged racial appeals in different wrappings, white students who fled public schools, and citizens who clung ever more defensively to their traditional racial views [313–314].

This is the South that I remember when I was growing up in the 1970s and 1980s — a culture of confusion, where one person may tell you one thing and another person something completely opposite, or where one person may make two statements that could never be reconciled with logic. A same interest in the total picture and those multicultural ideals inclined me to collect the stories included in *Children of the Changing South*.

The next work, Fred Hobson's *But Now I See: The White Southern Racial Conversion Narrative*, published seven years earlier in 1999, explores earlier examples of changing mentalities in the non-stereotypical Southern white people through his commentary on the lives and works of eight white Southern writers whose ideas about race as adults represented a conscious rejection of established Southern ideas of the time. This book focuses on memoirs by white writers alone who, like the writer of the hymn "Amazing Grace" (from which the book takes its title), repented of their racialized past and sought a better road to travel, one free of the South's deeply entrenched racism. After his examination of such famed Southern literary writers as Lillian Smith, Will Campbell and Willie Morris, Hobson punctuates his work, in the final chapter titled "Curious Intersections: Race and Class at Century's End," with a discussion of more modern conversion narratives by younger writers who do not risk the severity of consequences that earlier writers did. He writes first of memoirs in a newer South:

The memoirs [of recent decades] proliferated as a new mythology, seemingly at odds with the old racial benightedness, came to be associated with Dixie — not after 1980, the old mythology grounded in the realities of southern defeat, poverty, failure and general backwardness but rather the mythology of the Sun Belt with its gleaming new cities, resort "properties," Olympian success, political victories (two presidents in two decades), and general prosperity and optimism — a South, that is, no longer so noticeably haunted by God and not seeming to take sin and guilt *or* redemption so seriously as it earlier had [120–121].

and then:

...I also wondered if, despite the continuing streams of southern self-explo-ration, the new southern confessional literature would demonstrate the same urgency and intensity as the old writing, if it would be written from "the same mixture of love and anger, shame and pride" [121].

Unfortunately, Hobson concludes that he doubts that the "contemporary" writer is able to do so, because the risk is not inherent, not so pressing, nor looming, nor threatening. He almost seems to lament the by-gone days as a hopelessly lost contributing factor to a body of great literature, lamenting the loss of the "tortured old Dixie that is much more compelling, more exciting, than anything in the sanitized New South..." (121).

One of most difficult challenges of compiling *Children of the Changing South* was a prevailing notion that what-happened-next is not only not as "compelling" or "exciting," but that it is somehow not even worthy of discussion. While I will not argue with the "exciting" argument — the number of threats and actual violent incidents decrease dramatically after 1968 — I do take exception with the idea that these stories are not "compelling." While the contributions in this book vary widely in scope, focus, setting, and voice, each one provides for the reader a glimpse into a unique set of experiences that are important pieces of the Southern patchwork, all with the unifying feature of a retrospective look at childhood confusion. The memoir that details the earliest dates chronologically carries the reader from a girlhood in racially oppressive pre–Civil Rights Mississippi into a womanhood in post–Civil Rights Georgia and yields surprises in both the beginning and the end, while the latest memoir spends only a short time in the South, in Louisiana in the 1980s, but then carries its reader right up to the present day when the writers' Southern experience works its way into the election of the country's first African-American president.

While only one work in this collection deals in the threat of overt violence — a bomb threat at an all-black high school — the "compelling" ideas here are more subtle, more nuanced, much like the not-so-"sanitized New South." In this collection, the what-happens-next is retrospective contemplation by the adults who are conscientious participants in the modern South, and their diversity is no hindrance, but an even more intriguing reason for further examination.

Although Fred Hobson did seem to belittle newer writers for the lack of "excitement" in post–Civil Rights white conversion narratives, I do not subscribe to his idea that a lack of dangerous social tightrope-walking denigrates the importance of the ideas expressed in any post–Civil Rights narratives. As a counter-argument, I offer a theoretical basis in multicultural literary thought that Laurie Grobman writes about in her 2007 book *Multicultural Hybridity*:

> Literary texts arise out of specific, historical, cultural and rhetorical moments, and all writers are social constituted as well, fashioning their words through the languages of their many cultural affiliations. Yet, writers are not merely written by language; they consciously and deliberately use language to produce meaning, to create beauty, and to offer transformative aesthetic, social, and political visions. However, no writer is in complete control of his or her text's meaning, nor can a text's meaning(s) be located by discovering a writer's intentions: writing is both a product of its author experiences as socially constituted human beings and their deliberate choices as to how they might within or outside them [36].

Grobman's multicultural approach, which asserts that each writer is what he or she is and that each text is what it is, stands in direct opposition to Hobson's assertion that one set of writers or texts have somehow produced superior expressions that are more worthy of attention. While the great risks involved with, for instance, white progressives of the mid-twentieth century are evident, that acknowledgment of greater risk in no way denigrates the meaningful nature of the expressions of later writers.

These recent developments in scholarship on and interest and in Southern (and multicultural) topics underpin the meaningful nature of the memoirs in this collection. Where the Ole Miss symposium exhibits a critical understanding of the importance of listening not only to the stories of the adults during a historical period, but also its children, and where Blake's book shows a willingness to seek the children's versions of the most prominent stories, this collection builds upon those mantels and explores the subject in its own way. Furthermore, where Jason Sokol's heavily researched book exhibits a critical understanding of listening not only to black ideas and stories but also to white ideas and stories, and where Fred Hobson's book takes a deep look into a few prominent white voices of the earlier period, the writers of this collection represent an array of expressions and ideas, which when added together in one place can also offer a collective meaning about the children of the times.

Furthermore, in a multicultural discussion, there is a necessity to counterbalance my discussion of Hobson's and Sokol's explorations of white responses to the racial strife with African-American responses to situation being left behind. By resisting an essentialist view of responses to the changes that are the subject and background of this collection, acknowledging the complexity of African-American responses is equally important. Certainly, Southern culture has had its share of identity crises with subsequent socio-political actions that followed, but it is false to believe that all of the old ways are completely gone, as it would be false to believe that the old ways did not have a profound on the children of the past and the present. New South historians and critics were not needed to point out that fact.

The dehumanizing effects of slavery, segregation and Jim Crow are well-documented phenomena. One writer who openly acknowledged this fact was James Haskins in his "The Humanistic Black Heritage of Alabama," which was published in a 2002 collection of memoirs, *The Remembered Gate: Memoirs by Alabama Writers*:

> But to blacks like myself, who were born before World War II, the word *human* has a very important meaning. It was not for me, not for the other people whose names I have just listed, a quality or a state of being that could be taken for granted at all. For the major part of our history here in America, we black people have not been accorded by our fellow inhabitants of this continent full membership in the human race [54].

Haskins's words sum up one set of sentiments that many African-American writers felt, from Phyllis Wheatley whose imitative poetry, which contained a longing for the after-life to be better than this earthly one, to W.E.B. DuBois, who has written famously about the "double consciousness" whereby African Americans have had to live with two personalities at once, the one they show to white people and their real personality.

Another African-American writer, Jack Hunter O'Dell, wrote the following passages within a longer work titled "Notes on the Movement: Then, Now, and Tomorrow," which was published in *Southern Exposure* magazine in 1981, and later anthologized in the 1992 collection, *Black Southern Voices*:

> The laws were a crystallized form of expressing the new reality that people would no longer abide by the rules and mores of racial segregation. Segregation was in fact abolished by the power of the Civil Rights Movement. A movement, whether reform or revolution, always struggles for a legislative manifestation of its victory because that establishes a new code of conduct in relation to the old order of things. It confirms that change has been accepted and that the particular struggle for democracy has been victorious.
>
> Once the victory is formalized, the movement must regroup around the definition of the next stage of mass democracy and move on to its fulfillment. The opposition will inevitable attempt to trap the movement into preoccupying itself with implementing victories that have been codified into law [444].

In this reflection on the post-movement years, O'Dell discusses the difficult nature of what-happens-next. As the movement was forced to evolve by its own victories, the matter at hand became how to focus on continued efforts at equality and justice without simply resting on their laurels. Now that the legislative obstacles had been removed, the problem of making the changes a reality stood before them. The movement did not simply stop when "victory" had been achieved.

This fact leads to another component of *Children of the Changing South* being a modern view of the South: the issue of dates as historical demarcation points for a supposed end of the movement. After more than a decade of the bloody clashes and mass demonstrations both for and against a new way of living in America, Southern life was changed significantly after 1968, when Martin Luther King, Jr., was assassinated. Many end-dates are proffered as the end of the Civil Rights Movement (while more than a few people argue that the movement for social justice is still going strong today). The most commonly used paradigms employ either the *Brown v. Board* decision in 1954 or Rosa Parks' refusal to leave her seat on a Montgomery bus in 1955 as the beginning of the movement with the murders of King and Robert Kennedy, both in 1968, supplying a demarcation for the end. However, the more complex truth of the matter is that the struggle did not end when King and Kennedy died.

However, many Southerners understand the real-life impact of the changes in a more down-to-earth way that defies the altruisms about major events, the generalities of summaries, and the finality of historical demarcation dates. The changes brought on by the Civil Rights Movement, the Women's movement, and other trends have occurred in a slow evolution that did not simply stop in 1968, and scholars' treatments of the twentieth century South reflect that understanding. One example is a work I have already alluded to, historian Numan V. Bartley's 1995 book, *The New South, 1945–1980: The Story of the South's Modernization*, which creates a narrative with a longer view that lumps together the time period from the end of World War II to the election of Ronald Reagan in creating an image of how the modern South came to be.

In two recently published books on specific facets of the Civil Rights Movement, *Carry It On: The War on Poverty and the Civil Rights Movement in Alabama, 1964–1972* by Susan Youngblood Ashmore and *Bloody Lowndes: Civil Rights and Black Power in Alabama's Black Belt* by Hasan Kwame Jeffries, the examination of the movement's work and effects carries on beyond 1968. Ashmore's study obviously (from the subtitle) follows the events all the way to 1972 with a final chapter entitled "Old Patterns and New Designs," and Jeffries' work ends with a final chapter titled, "Now Is the Time for Work to Begin: Black Politics in the Post-Civil Rights Era" and an epilogue titled, "The Black Dirt Gets in Your Soul: The Fight for Freedom Rights in Days Ahead." Unlike the traditional and most popular narratives, as in David J. Garrow's voluminous 1986 book, *Bearing the Cross: Martin Luther King and the Southern Christian Leadership Conference*, which ends its narrative in Memphis in 1968 with King's bloody murder, more recent writers on Southern history are taking the discussion beyond King's death, and even beyond King himself, beyond the 1960s, and some even into the present day. I also take this longer view: while acknowledging that historians and other scholars need major events as clear markers for their work, the spirit of the equality movements of the 1950s and 1960s did not end in the late 1960s, even if their forms changed, or even if we choose to regard the 1970s and 1980s as the *post*–Civil Right movement years, in the same way that artistic movements like *Post*-Impressionism and *Post*-Modernism are understood as direct outcroppings of their respective predecessors.

Other facts also support this multicultural view of how the movement continued and morphed in the years after Martin Luther King, Jr.'s death. During and after the movement years, the historical dichotomies were breaking down and the pluralist nature of a freer society was showing itself. Although his SNCC roots and his 1967 book *Black Power: The Politics of Liberation* both predated King's death, Stokely Carmichael's influence and ideas about the possibilities for African Americans' lives rippled out well into the 1970s and beyond. Another SNCC veteran, Harvard-educated teacher Bob Moses tells his post-movement story in the 2001 book, *Radical Equations: Civil Rights from Mississippi to the Algebra Project*; Moses' Algebra Project, founded in 1982, emphasizes math education, especially in low-income schools, as a key to having a strong economic future. Furthermore, the 1971 founding of the still-prominent Southern Poverty Law Center, whose programs have included Klan Watch and Teaching Tolerance, also shows a side of the continued necessity for attention to issues of inequality.

After children who witnessed the Southern changes of mid-century had begun growing into adulthood, it was into this latter-day social climate that Generation X was born, from the mid 1960s, when the Civil Rights Act of 1964, the Selma-to-Montgomery March, and the Voting Rights Act of 1965 were changing society, to about 1980, the year that Ronald Reagan was elected President of the United States. While the recollections and narratives of the writers with a childhood during the movement years are significant in describing the realities of growing up among turmoil, more than half of the contributors in this collection belong to Generation X and tell post-movement stories of the multicultural South. These latter-day writers explore their own narratives that are set during an entirely different kind of turmoil, the kind that occurred once the dust had settled (if it ever really did).

After the landmark events had occurred, after the major court rulings had been handed down, and as people began to learn a new multicultural way of living together, and the complexities that had to be addressed were staggering. Aside from striking down and repealing many local and state laws, Southerners both black and white had to change their fundamental ways of interacting with each other. Again, Sokol sums up the scenario well:

> For some, the law forced changes in practice, but it could not touch the recesses of hearts and minds. Others began to question deeply held views even though their lives looked much the same as before. At times, the old stereotypes and everyday practices died hard together. And for still others, change in any form — in law, mind-set, or lifestyle — was something to fear and resist, with denial and bitterness, all the way to the grave [15].

And if that was not enough, the Civil Rights Movement sparked other social movements, most prevalently among women, and when the social fabric changed so did the economic fabric, when more different types of people entered the workplaces previously dominated by white men.

As a member of Generation X myself, I also share those experiences. Our grandparents were products of the Depression and World War II, while our parents were products of the post-war and Civil Rights eras. My maternal grandmother was born on a farm in Lowndes County, Alabama, in 1911, and my maternal grandfather was from Virginia and served in the Navy during World War II. Then the parents of Generation X experienced the turmoil of the 1950s and 1960s firsthand, many of them as students in schools that were being integrated. In my family, again as examples, my parents both graduated from Sidney Lanier High School in Montgomery, Alabama, in 1964 and 1967, respectively; as a point of reference, Montgomery's school desegregation case, *Carr v. Montgomery Public Schools* was filed in 1964 and the city's last appeal lost in 1967, and the public schools in the "Cradle of the Confederacy" began to mix children of two races together under a federal court order. To frame the history in another way, my father was 19 and my mother 16, when the Selma-to-Montgomery March happened. Those of us lumped into Generation X were raised in a multicultural South. Yet our parents had been raised with racialized experiences that began during the time of segregation, and then with experiences of conflict and its pursuant climate of fear, then uncertainty, and finally with a stated goal of attempting to live together peacefully in the aftermath.

The variety of scenarios within the actions and reactions has been vast. Some white people had long used intimidation tactics, ranging from taunting to lynching, to keep black people in constant fear. Prior to the movement, most black people in the South lacked a substantial education and had few job skills beyond housekeeping or manual labor, which was one result of the Jim Crow system. Even white people who did not consider themselves racists were not accustomed to standing in a grocery store line with or sitting on a bus beside black people. In the black community, strategies to remedy the inequality ranged from militant to conservative, from organized to haphazard, from determined to frustrated. White reactions ranged from subtle to violent, from resentful to accommodating, from reluctance to acceptance. Black reactions ranged from thankful to resentful, from angry to elated, from humbled to celebratory. To believe that Martin Luther King marched and gave a speech and then everyone just went about their business in a kinder, gentler South would be simple and foolish — the diversity of actions and reactions was immense.

One thing I have learned from the Civil Rights Movement is that movements are made up of *people*. If asked about the 1970s in the South, a historian might discuss the activities of the Ku Klux Klan, the effects of Black Power, or the shooting of George Wallace. Those movements and events do provide an overview of how some factions within American culture became even more extreme, but ordinary people were trying to keep on living. Again using my own hometown of Montgomery as an example, three everyday repercussions of the Montgomery Bus Boycott were: it basically destroyed the public transit system in the city because many people stopped riding buses out of fear of possible confrontations; it caused "white flight" into new neighborhoods in the eastern part of the city and contributed to suburban sprawl; and it turned downtown into a ghost town as businesses left the proverbial battle zone and followed their white customers. Similar changes occurred in Montgomery, and all over the South, in the schools, when the rise of the "white academy system" emerged as a response to integrated schools. While no one will deny the valuable human rights progress of the Civil Rights Movement, few people discuss the aftermath, which also included as a consequence the failure of many black-owned businesses because their black customers could now shop anywhere they wanted, and what they often wanted was the white-owned stores with better selection and lower prices.

Race is the most obvious topic in this discussion, but there is so much more to explore in the additional areas of gender roles, social class, and political affiliations. In addition to trying to make sense of where people of this or that race fit into society, this concurrent social movement questioned traditional ideas about the role of women in society, in the family, and in the workplace. Understanding that the South is quite conservative socially, having two national movements occurring almost simultaneously fell heavily on the South's white supremacist, patriarchal culture. The white male in the South found himself at war on two fronts. If this was not enough pressure on a culture that prided itself on the "colonial" ideals of domination and extraction, these new roles in the areas of race and gender affected class issues too, as educational and career opportunities for black people and women increased, catapulting them into contention for jobs, political offices, and social standing traditionally held only by white men. If it was not enough pressure on these men to deal with the racial changes in their lives outside the home, they faced another revolution when they got home.

It is this climate that the contributors in *Children of the Changing South* experienced as children and that they have now offered to share as their stories.

Summation

This collection, *Children of the Changing South*, is a small sampling of memoirs about eighteen people's experiences of the sweeping social changes of mid-century, and what came after, from the late 1950s until early 1990s. These stories, through written by the adults, are recalled by people who witnessed those times as children. The young people of this time period lived their formative years when no one was really sure what was acceptable anymore. Parents who had largely attended segregated schools were now attending racially mixed PTA meetings and teacher conferences. For the first time in some places, African-American police officers patrolled the streets, answered disturbance calls, and made arrests. As children, we — black and white alike — heard lamentations about the good old days and the way things used to be, but we had no knowledge or experience of that way of living.

Children of the Changing South is not just another piece of the Civil Rights Movement puzzle. First, the memoirs included in this collection are more literary in style than historical; although a few of the writers included here are historians, most are literary writers. The South has a well-established tradition of examining its own culture from the viewpoints of children. Within the genre of fiction, Harper Lee's *To Kill a Mockingbird* cuts to the core of the Depression-era Southern small town and does so through a loss-of-innocence framework narrative, in which Scout Finch's naïve voice tells the story; in Carson McCullers' *The Heart is a Lonely Hunter*, readers experience another Southern small town through another tomboy protagonist, Mick Kelly; and William Faulkner's story "Barn Burning" uses its young male protagonist to delve into the mind and motives of his unscrupulous father, a poor white sharecropper. In the genre of nonfiction, the joint memoir *Selma, Lord, Selma* by Sheyann Webb and Rachel West Nelson, relays their experiences of growing up amidst the events of the Selma-to-Montgomery March in 1965. As people grow up, they often attempt to make sense of their formative years, and although Southerners do not have a monopoly on this trend, there is a tradition of literature based on these reminiscences.

In the February 2009 issue of the *Oxford American*, which was devoted to race, editor Mark Smirnoff wrote in his introductory piece that Montaigne derived the term essay from the word meaning "to attempt." I was glad to read Smirnoff's words as I was working on this book, because even about forty years after what most people consider the end of the movement we are only now really *attempting* to have modern Southern culture make sense.

In another insightful book about Southern memoirs, *Tell About the South: The Southern Rage to Explain*, Fred Hobson (also the author of *But Now I See*) examines and analyzes the need by some Southern white writers of the past to write about the deepest emotions, ideas, and anxieties of their cultural predicament. These intellectual points of reference for this book are texts that I also encountered only recently, while compiling this book. *Tell About the South: The Southern Rage to Explain*, which was published in 1983, is a literary study on twelve Southern writers from the mid–1800s to mid–1900s who focused their work on what the South is and what it means to be a Southerner. Hobson wrote that Southerners are more prone to "self-examination" and "explanation" than people from other regions of the country because we feel like we have something to explain about ourselves and our culture — thus, his subtitle — either as an "apologist" who defends the South or as a "native critic" who attacks the actions and events of the past. Although Hobson's earlier book examines Southern writers of the past, he ends his prologue by writing:

> The Southern confessional literature will no doubt continue, partly because the South, whatever its changes, is still distinctive and picturesque. But one

questions, again, whether the new confessional literature will be written from
the same mixture of love and anger, shame and pride, whether an all-
consuming passion to explain will constitute the basis for Southern writing as
it did for that of Ruffin and Dabney, Davidson and Cash. The confessional
literature has already become in part, one suspects, a habit in the South, a
function, an aesthetic ritual. The young creative Southerner who leaves his
home now writes the obligatory confessional because his predecessors have
[15].

From this literary tradition the memoirs in *Children of the Changing
South* have come, not from the tradition of politically charged and/or
activist pronouncements that fill works like Howell Raines' *My Soul Is
Rested*.

　　Another knowledgeable commentary comes in a bit of reportage that
appeared in *Newsweek* in August 1970, titled "The South Revisited after
a Momentous Decade," by writer Karl Fleming who describes the South
that he found after the movement's furious pace had slowed. Although he
begins his piece with a highly descriptive image-building style that borders
on stereotype, he moves within the article to checking up on former
hotbeds of the movement, like Montgomery, Selma, and Birmingham,
Alabama; Stone Mountain, Georgia; and Philadelphia, Mississippi, in
order to assess the effects, now that the 1960s were over. He begins his
final passage, his summation, with "And so it all has changed," then moves
on to something more tangible:

> The millennium is not yet: the white South still has all its old genius for
> altering matters of etiquette and still preserving the subtle arrangements of
> color and caste and distance. Some of the towns I visited were rushing into
> private schools they can't really afford; others have contrived to integrate their
> schools and segregate their classrooms as rigidly as ever. One evening in Jack-
> son, two fiery young black women lectured me at passionate length to the
> effect that nothing is different, nothing is better and that the black revolution
> is coming [846].

　　Forty years after Fleming's jaunt through the South, some of his statements could still be regarded as true. I offer that the stories in *Children of
the Changing South* are compelling for the same reason that the range of
ideas and reactions is evident in this passage by Fleming. Furthermore, the
notion that the tensions just evaporated is far too naïve and oversimplified
and rests on the rhetoric of some post–Civil Rights leaders who wanted it
to seem that way, in order to attempt to build yet another un–Recon-
structed New South.
　　As scholars and critics now debate where we are now as a society —

one catalyst being the election of America's first African-American president, Barack Obama, in November 2008 — the complexity of the question is abundantly evident. With perhaps greater clarity than ever, we are beginning to admit how we have not yet dealt with race as an issue, as in Attorney General Eric Holder's 2009 comment that we are "a nation of cowards" when it comes to discussing race. We are beginning to understand how inextricably race, gender, and social class are interlinked, as evidenced in the confirmation hearings of new Supreme Court Justice Sonya Sotomayor. We are beginning to face how subjugated groups in America are denied economic benefits, which then affects their political standing. We are beginning to discuss openly how education and material success are related. We are beginning to realize how we were duped and held back by skilled rhetoricians who used race to cloud the public understanding of real progress. Many writers have speculated about what would happen to the South if change were to come, while others who were there to witness it have attempted to describe and assess it. Of course, I have already alluded to W. J. Cash's idea that the South was about to have to realize its "capacity for adjustment."

The focus of *Children of the Changing South* is not to answer these big questions, but what it will do is contribute to a new set of narratives. As they say: Let's start at the beginning. Today, those of us who were children from the 1950s through 1980s are now adults who spend at least some of our time reflecting with maturity on our earliest experiences. Like so much of life, many things we encounter during this backtracking make no sense, while the real nature of other situations has become clear. Each writer in this collection takes on some aspect of his or her own past, an attempts to navigate the muddy waters.

The Memoirs

Children of the Changing South approaches a different issue of the recent South. The anthology is a collection of memoirs, which are literary works, not of scholarly historical analyses. The South has a long and rich tradition of literature — both in nonfiction and in fiction — whose narrators look back on childhood, loss of innocence, or coming to terms with the past: *To Kill a Mockingbird* by Harper Lee, *The Heart Is a Lonely Hunter* by Carson McCullers, or a plethora of short stories such as the ones collected in anthologies like *Growing Up in the South: An Anthology of Modern Southern Literature*— so the themes here are not new. However, regarding

them as both a continuation of a tradition and as products of a newer and
very different South is not irreconcilable.

The nonfiction works included in this collection involve the telling
of the significant memories by unaffiliated writers whose experiences with
a childhood in the South span five decades — the 1950s, 1960s, 1970s, 1980s
and 1990s — during which many changes occurred. Because the stories are
narrated by adults, but relay the experiences of children or with children,
the added burden of a moral assessment is *less* necessary than it would be
for the story of an someone who was an adult during these times. These
childhood stories are often about confusion, ambivalence or interrogation,
rather than justification, moral rightness or self-defense.

Beginning the collection's rough chronology, Jacqueline Wheelock
tells a story of her youth spent in the pre–Civil Rights Movement years
in Mississippi, which carries over into her adult years as a teacher in Georgia
in the 1970s, where she interacts with youth in a different context. Wheelock's narrative takes the reader back to 1958, just as the movement was
beginning, after *Brown v. Board* and the Montgomery Bus Boycott, but
before Little Rock, the Sit-Ins and the Freedom Rides. However, Wheelock
begins there in order to make three very important points: first, that even
poor white people thought nothing of the ill treatment of any black people;
second, that a strong African-American woman like her mother felt no
compulsion to yield to the Jim Crow social system when her child had
been mistreated; and third, that times had changed very much from her
1950s girlhood to her teaching career in the 1970s. The strength of her
story also lies in a picture of change, for herself and for her white students
and their parents later on. What Wheelock has to say about her students
may be just as telling as what she says about herself.

The importance of Jacqueline Wheelock's narrative can be summed
up by the three elements in her title, "Power," "Love" and a "Sound Mind."
Early in the story, her mother's love saves her from a cruel situation within
a Jim Crow social scenario: the white woman who had employed this child
as temporary help would not even stop to let her eat or drink or rest, and
a mother's love for her child transcended even the rigid social codes of the
day, as we see an African-American woman stand up to a white man.
Beyond that, as a teacher, Wheelock's love for her students allowed that
group of children in the post–Civil Rights period to look beyond their
teacher's race and reciprocate that love in a way that startled their own
parents. In these scenes, "Power, Love and a Sound Mind" provides two
different examples of the complex nature of Southern life and childhood,
where even well-known rules had exceptions.

Lean'tin Bracks' story then carries the reader further into the movement years than Wheelock's memoir, but further back than where Wheelock ends up. Bracks' story of community and fear, set in 1964, brings the collection's focus back to a time before the harmoniously (or politely?) integrated scene that Wheelock describes, and it shows a contrast. Bracks' story is set in a time of great turmoil for the South, the year after the Sixteenth Street Baptist Church bombing, the year of the Civil Rights Act and Freedom Summer, and the year before the Selma-to-Montgomery Voting Rights March and the subsequent Voting Rights Act. Set in an unnamed Southern town, "Covered Walkways" provides a snapshot of a Southern black community that is rocked by a bomb threat to its school, and consequently to its children. As a result of the bombing in Birmingham that killed four girls, the bomb threats were taken very seriously, and Bracks explains to her reader how this traumatic event — being threatened with death by someone who she did not know and who would not identify himself — shaped her consciousness.

Jim Grimsley, Lillie Anne Brown, and Becky McLaughlin move the collection into the later years of the movement and tell three very different stories of school integration. First, in "Black Bitch," Jim Grimsley, a white writer who was raised in North Carolina, provides a treatment of his experiences with black students entering his previously all-white elementary school class and gives the reader a glimpse into how young people reacted when faced with the inevitable confusion linked to contact with others unlike them, others they may have been told are inferior or worse. Jim Grimsley provides no outright date for his story, and consequently creates a narrative that could have taken place anywhere in the South during a wide span of time, and likely did. Because school integration often came in the form of initially trickling only a few black students into white schools, overwhelming experiences existed for both sides: with black students being keenly aware how massively outnumbered they were and with white students navigating the space between basic classroom decorum and the discomfiting presence of black students.

The portrayal of confusion here is rooted in the combination of childish innocence and the anticipation of meanness. "Black Bitch" creates a scenario where no answer can be the right answer for a white boy who does not wish to be in the presence of a black girl and moreover does not want to be undone her, especially in front of everyone. This memoir shows the changing dynamics of race relations in an integrated school setting. We have no indication that Theona is frightened or worried in her new surroundings, especially when she declares that she is "proud" about her

race and who she is. As the narrator navigates the nuanced meanings of
racial pejoratives — nigger, Negro, niggra — he is as unsure of what to do
as Theona seems sure of what to do. In our modern consciousness where
the generalizations about integration are ones of fearful black students trying merely to make it through the day, Theona Bragg stands in stark contrast in Grimsley's story. However, we must be careful in reading "Black
Bitch" not to assume that we know what Theona is thinking or feeling,
what may be driving her actions, despite what she portrays outwardly.

Lillie Anne Brown's "Conversion" then explores another side of the
situation described by Jim Grimsley. Brown tells her story of being a black
high school student in the class of a white teacher who seems to be trying
too hard to ingratiate the new black students and does so in a most inappropriate manner. Brown's story and its commentary looks at what may
be a white adult overtaken by fear or what may the overweening pride of
a white liberal; as we can't assume anything about Theona Bragg, we also
can't say for sure what the truth about the teacher is, and neither can
Brown. Set in 1969 in Tallahassee, Florida, "Conversion" tells a very Southern story in a place that some people do not consider as a part of "the
South." However, Florida's school desegregation story was classically
Southern, with its roots in the 1954 *Brown v. Board* case and its slow plod-
ding pace that carried its final stages into the 1970s. Brown tells her reader
that 1969 was the third year of integrated classes at her Tallahassee high
school, where her history class was somewhat mysteriously "nearly all-
black."

The tension in "Conversion" lies in its pitting of a white history
teacher who is overly anxious to repeat the fact of the glorious Emancipation Proclamation to her only recently integrated class versus an African-
American young woman with a budding interest in the writings of powerful
African-American writers like Eldridge Cleaver, W.E.B. DuBois, and
Richard Wright, as well as the consciousness-raising Frantz Fanon. In the
story, Mrs. Byrd can easily represent the precariously cautious white liberal,
whose moderate views are shown through the extolling of safer topics like
the freeing of slaves more than a hundred years earlier at the same she
subtly decries a reading of Wright's *Black Boy* by saying " put away all that
stuff and listen to me." Brown's voice alternately represents the carefully
reflective woman looking back on a time that no one knew the proper
thing to do or say. School integration was very real by 1969, but so was
the consternation of white teachers who faced roomfuls of African-
American students, some of whom were engaging powerfully pro-Black
ideas, and so was the soul-searching of a generation of African-American

young people with new access to a new racial pride and the voices that endorsed it; both James Brown's song, "Black and Proud" and Eldridge Cleaver's book, *Soul on Ice*, came out in 1968, the year before Lillie Anne Brown's experiences that are described in this narrative. Not only is "Conversion" a story of racial struggle, it is also about generational struggles.

Moving onto a different focus, Becky McLaughlin is the first writer in the collection to explore one aspect of what is often called "the white man's burden." In "Growing Up Out of Place," she deals first with her own sense of being an "Other" as a white child of missionary parents in Africa and again later within her native Southern culture where white people like herself held the dominant positions. McLaughlin's family, who were Christian missionaries, darted in and out of the South while she was a child. Having been born in a small town in Arkansas, then taken to the Belgian Congo from around ages four to seven, only to be brought back to Arkansas in 1967 when school integration was taking full effect, McLaughlin's perspective on the world was different than most of the children (and adults) around her. Beginning her narrative with a discussion of Lillian Smith's *Killers of the Dream*, in which Smith writes about the spurious connections between being a Southerner in the segregated South and being a Christian, carries the story of this tenuous bond into real life experiences, when the author is faced over a span of years with hearing her sister use the N-word in a child's rhyme, with a naïve questioning about who she will marry, with attending a liberal church that favors integration, with reacting to a high school friend's racist joke.

The reflections of Becky McLaughlin attempt to explain a childhood response to a similar phenomena that Fred Hobson explored in the adult writers featured in *But Now I See ...* McLaughlin was raised not to and chose not to take part in the typical Southern racism of her surroundings, including attending a church whose minister favored integration, and the situations that she encountered as a result stand out among stereotypes of Southern life. She recollects knowing better than taking part in vulgarity or pettiness, even as a child; however, the stark contrasts between the races still stood as an impediment to full and equal engagement, as seen in her examination of the litmus test in being asked, "did you know you marry the person you sit next to in school?" by an African-American classmate who sat near her, or when she has to ask herself if she does not allow racism to drive her decision not to allow a black classmate to cheat off her paper. "Growing Up Out of Place" shows the reader one side of the confusion in the heart and mind of a child who is not participating in the cultural norms of the day.

Next, in "Women's Work and Working Women," Leslie Haynsworth is the first writer in the collection to focus directly on women's roles in the South and we see some ways that the racial struggles and women's struggles were intertwined. Haynsworth, who is white and grew up in South Carolina, discusses her own life alongside the peripheral issues involved with her own mother, her family's housekeeper, and her African-American students. Her story weaves through many issues that interconnect: the effects of primary and secondary education on the possibilities of success in post-secondary education, the availability of child care for young women seeking more education, the changes in both opportunities and attitudes among African-American women, and the willingness of educators to work with women who are trying to raise children and get an education. Acknowledging that some careers — teaching and nursing, for example — require a college degree, the issue of educational opportunities and the feasibility of accepting those opportunities takes the forefront in this work.

The recognition of interlaced social stigma provides a rationale for the importance of Leslie Haynsworth's memoir in this collection. She taps into a very important aspect of Southern culture, at what may seem like a less important moment in the work: in discussing her father-in-law, she contrasts him with her own mother who has rejected ingrained racism and made conscious choices against it, by making him a symbol of something larger: "I've never heard him say anything overtly racist. But it's clear to me that for him certain accoutrements of racism appear both natural and desirable." The looming specter behind all of Haynsworth's explanations is the "natural and desirable" benefit for many white people — both men and women — of keeping African-Americans, especially women, locked into certain roles. The author herself acknowledges how much easier her own life, work, and career might have been if she had had her own Bessie, someone there to handle the inconvenient, daily domestic work. However, an evolution has taken place, and although the dire circumstances that many people live with have not subsided entirely, the situation, Haynsworth acknowledges, has changed for the better.

The next work in the collection, "1975 Wasn't a Very Good Year" by Georgene Bess Montgomery, builds its narrative around a different premise of changes that are constructed out of self-empowerment. Raised near Glenwood, Georgia, a rural area in the southwestern portion of the state, her family was African-American farmers. Built around the year in the mid–1970s when the author's father dies, this narrative has roots that go further back into an archetypal Southern upbringing that commingled idyllic fun, hard farm work, close-knit families, and constant fear and intimidation at the hands of white people. However, significant changes were on the horizon. Montgomery and her siblings attended the all-black Wheeler County Training School, until the schools became integrated in the early 1970s when she was in elementary school. Montgomery's story of the classic rural South, complete with combating bigotry and fear, is one of witnessing changes in people, even the most stalwart ones.

Montgomery's memoir is a powerful story of experiencing her formative years during a time of intense change, and its importance lies in showing the complexity of altered Southern communities. As the story begins, we receive a description of the conflicts that surround an African-American man trying to buy land, for instance, and what his family goes through — poisoned livestock and groups of white men hanging ominously around their yard late at night — after his strong presence is removed. As in Jacqueline Wheelock's story, we also see a strong mother figure, Sarah, whose love for her children outweighs any outward hesitancy about standing up to white people, even regarding the racist bus driver who is eventually shunned by the wider community. As the story progresses, and the process of integration is in motion, we are not surprised by the tales of unkindness and even cruelty. However, Montgomery ends with a portrait of her hometown, years later, when she is greeted and welcomed by the self-same people who had been so abusive. The strength of "1975 Wasn't A Very Good Year" is evidenced by its dual portrayals of the things we expect to see and the things we do not.

In "The Absence of Water," poet Glenis Redmond takes the reader on a personal tour-de-force that explores the precarious relationships of African Americans to water, of race to vacationing, of mothers to their children, and of poetry to healing. Dancing in and out of seemingly unrelated topics, including her own battles with Fibromyalgia, Redmond takes a poetic look at her own life in the South as both a child herself and as a woman raising children in the South. Although Redmond did not spend her whole childhood in the South, the Southern-ness of her parents' Jim Crow upbringing in South Carolina had hung like a pall over her own life, as their attitudes and habits dictated a way of life. As the piece intersperses poetry with nuanced memoir, "The Absence of Water" carries the reader through examining and eventually overcoming a fear of water that was based on the family's lack of access to vacationing, thus to recreational swimming, and makes the journey through levels of family and the post–Civil Rights era South.

What Redmond shows us in this work is the definite of impact of parents, who grew up during a segregated time, trying to raise children after Jim Crow had fallen, and consequently how those children would grow to live their own lives and raise their own children. It is equally important to recognize the symbolism in the title, "The Absence of Water," because water is most significantly here a symbol of access to a better life, i.e. vacations, but it is also the life-giving element on the planet Earth; nothing can live without water. Glenis Redmond grew up with an "absence of water," but tells a story that shows how she learned to overcome that lack of access to a better life, through marrying interracially, through taking her own children to the beach, and through utilizing water as a treatment for her fibromyalgia. It can be said that poetry is an art form of transcendence that allows the poet to weave through experiences in an unfetter way to come to necessary conclusions; although only some of this work is written in verse, "The Absence of Water" weaves through the obstacles in that way.

Stephanie Powell Watts' "Black Power"* examines her own situation, one similar in ways to that of Glenis Redmond, as she grew up in North Carolina in the 1970s. However, unlike Redmond's narrative that creates an image of her parents as somewhat paralyzed by their earlier Jim Crow, "Black Power" paints a different picture of her own father's and aunt's memories of the all-black school. Watts weaves together two sets of experiences, both revolving around being African-American in the South: riding a bus with other black children to the now-closed Freedman High School to receive the inoculation for sickle cell anemia and listening to her father and aunt explain the heyday of their alma mater. She explains being a black student in an integrated school system where she is one of relatively few black students. Watts' recollections of her father's enthusiasm for music and his storytelling and of how something we often think of as silly and culturally low — a cheerleader's cheer — brings her into the joy of her parents' world of the past, as she looks on "[m]ore black kids than I had ever seen in my life" congregated at the old school — a site of past black pride — in a whole new social scene.

Watts' "Black Power" very effectively makes important connections between her own past to the past of her family, her own life to the wider cultural milieu of the 1970s, and, near the end of the piece, her own present to her formative years. By using her own bus ride as the outer frame of her overall narrative, we are allowed into two sets of memories, what was the narrator's present and what constituted her heritage. The pieces of the stories from her father and aunt make it possible for us to witness a tiny

*First published in the Oxford American as "Finding Black Power," no. 64 (February 2010).

portion of a more human side of all-black schools, away from the political explanations of inequality, to know a little more about the *real lives* of the students in those schools, which seem here far from dreary. Watts' also carries us into how even rural children of 1970s South were not cut off from the popular culture of the day: watching the actress Cicely Tyson or listening to Paul McCartney's music. Finally, in a poignant ending to "Black Power," Watts' assesses some of the meanings in her narrative, telling us that she now teaches and lives in a majority-white scenario, and "[t]here's nothing with any of that," she assures us, but that "togetherness" is what matters. This conclusion — that nothing can sever her from a past to which she feels connected — carries us, her readers, for a moment, into Southern, African-American history of the 1970s and back out again to the present to reflect.

Camika C. Spencer's "1987 Tenth Grade" moves the collection's focus out of the 1970s and into the 1980s, and takes a hard look at subsequent issues of race, suburban flight, and public education in the post–Civil Rights South. Spencer, who is African American, grew up in Texas, and when her parents divorced, her father moved to the nearly all-white suburb of Lancaster while her mother remained in Dallas. Spencer attended school in Lancaster for junior high, but when her father moved, she was returned to Dallas to attended South Oak Cliff High School, which was commonly known as the "School of Crime," she explains. She also explains that the school had changed from nearly all-white in 1965 to nearly all black by 1970, and that by the time her brother had attended there, discipline was so out of hand that he skipped one of his classes every day for six weeks without a word being spoken of it, much to their mother's chagrin. Spencer gives us a tour the "School of Crime" through her memories of trying to get registered on her first day and also through an intense scene on a bus ride home with a substitute bus driver.

"1987 Tenth Grade" offers the reader several real-life examples of the changes that were occurring in the South by the 1980s: suburban flight, neighborhood re-segregation, divorce, and student-body make-up in inte-grated schools. As a child who was moved between households and schools as a result of her parents' divorce, Camika C. Spencer describes the two different lifestyles involved in navigating both communities. At an early point in the memoir, she discusses the type of "togetherness" that Stephanie Powell Watts touches on, in describing her early experiences where the whole community was raising the children. However, after three years in a peaceful white suburb, a different manner of difficulty arises:

Now, I was walking the halls of this school amongst my own people, not
wanting to get shot, robbed, or knocked up. I didn't have these types of
thoughts or concerns at Lancaster where a part of me feels I should have.
Sure, I wasn't excited about possibly being called a nigger, but I was prepared
to handle that on all fronts. Black-on-Black crime is another beast entirely.

The issues raised by her presentation of her urban high school in the 1980s
are very complex as we see the effects of changing cultures on the schools.
The portrayal involves more than race; it involves social and economic
realities, the dynamics of changing families, alterations to the nature of
neighborhoods and communities, and mostly the stark realization of how
the burdens were laid heaviest on the children who were being raised in
this new, splintered reality.

Where Camika C. Spencer explores the difficulties of the dualities of
suburb versus urban, nearly all-white homogeneity contrasted with the
all-black homogeneity, Anne Estepp's narrative discusses a completely different scenario: experiencing racial and social tensions within a culture of
all-white homogeneity. In "Why It Matters," Estepp describes her life,
growing up in Kentucky, where the homogeneous white population had
its subtle racism and where social class replaced race in the spectrum of
difference. Estepp's narrative centers on how racial issues, specifically those
dealing with African Americans, were handled like the proverbial elephant
in the room. In a town where no African Americans lived, her only knowledge of them was through popular culture — TV and music — but when
she brought the issue home, it was not received well in a household that
had forbidden the use of the N-word. When she inquired about her father's
distinct features, his darker skin and wavy hair, she was met with outright
resistance to the idea that there may be African blood in her family lineage,
possibly from African-American "scabs" used to break United Mine Workers strikes.

Anne Estepp's memoir highlights an important distinction to be made
about this subject of growing up in the South: there is not *one* essentialist
Southern experience anymore than there is *one* South. The mountains of
Kentucky contain a different culture, a different population, than for
instance the Deep South states like Alabama and Mississippi. With the
common conception of the South as a region having keen racial tensions,
Estepp's work prompts the question, in what form does that racism manifest when no non-white people live in the area or anywhere near it?
Hoskins tells us that at a young age she had never seen an African-American
person and later in the work that she realized that no Native Americans
had lived near her home for centuries. Social class may have replaced race

as a distinguishing factor where she lives, prompting the tension to take on another form, but a consciousness of race clearly continued to exist. What begins as a recollection of a very young children's rhyme — the same one that appears in Becky McLaughlin's memoir — weaves around the popular culture of the 1980s and returns eventually to history, to family, and to a re-assessment of one's own self.

The next five memoirs hold us in the Deep South, in the state of Alabama, during the 1980s and early 1990s. All five examine, each in its own way, some aspect of a more modern time when racism took less overt forms, when the questions outnumbered the answers, and when answers were often even withheld. As the ember of the Civil Rights Movement had dimmed significantly in the public consciousness by the 1980s, it is still important to remember that the tension was not gone. As examples of the tensions of the 1980s and 1990s, controversies over Confederate flags flying on top of Southern state capitols and the continued re-election of South Carolina's Sen. Strom Thurmond, whose role in the Dixiecrat Party and vehement support of segregation in the 1950s had not caused him to lose any elections, showed that old ideals were not completely gone. One severe example of the ever-present element that racism had remained was the 1981 lynching of Michael Donald by two Ku Klux Klansmen in Mobile, Alabama.

Ashley Day's story in "The Difference" explains growing up without ingrained racism, even being forbidden from it. As she describes being raised by parents and family who were as Southern as any in this collection, we see the "togetherness" that Stephanie Powell Watts wrote about and the idyllic fun and games that Georgene Bess Montgomery wrote about. However, Day, who is white, had parents who were clear about the predilections against the kinds of intolerance that were prevalent in the Deep South during the 1970s and 1980s: an ambivalent mistrust of something undefined, something foreign, something that smacks of racism. As Day explains her upbringing, which created in her a distinct consciousness about the sensitive matters of race and class, she portrays for us a kind of people we have not yet seen in the memoirs so far — except for maybe in Becky McLaughlin's "Growing Up Out of Place — people who are *living in* the South, who are *of* the South, but who are not *typical of* the South. She ends "The Difference" by showing us a distinct difference between herself and her brother, whose mixed attitudes seem to exemplify ambivalence.

Remaining in Alabama, Dawne Shand recalls a space similar to that of Hoskins' and Day's memories, of experiences with the slippery slope of a complex Southern culture's notions of what is acceptable and what is not: Shand's "Hed: The Unwritten Rules" explores the problems of young people crossing racial lines, even for friendships, and the consequences for the people who do it. She begins in Selma, an epicenter of the Civil Rights Movement in the mid–1960s that had calmed back down into a sleepy town by the mid–1970s, where the questions of her schooling and of her mother's decisions were held to scrutiny. As Shand continues in a vignette style, we catch first a glimpse of a friendship with handsome African-American high school classmate, then a piece of conversation in which a boyfriend doesn't care about George Wallace or his stand, and later a date to a University of Alabama football game where the African-American homecoming queen is derided by members of the crowd, including one call to "Lynch her!" In Shand's memoir, it is not the plot but the tone that stands out, the collage-like building of an overall image. Her "unwritten rules" cannot be named completely or described clearly, but are understood in a more vague way where both the lines and the consequences are left thoroughly unclear about defying a new kind of racial code of behavior.

However deeply issues of race may be in Southern culture, issues of social class and gender are never far from the surface either. "Attempts to Bury History Backfire" by Kyes Stevens transports us to two small towns in Alabama, where old ways hold fast and old habits — no matter how illogical or outmoded — refuse to die. Stevens' story begins in Jasper, a nearly all-white area in the mining regions of northwestern Alabama, and later moves to the Auburn area in the eastern part of the state, specifically to the tiny community of Waverly. By focusing on the absurdity of petty squabbles and the insistence of some people to hone in on differences, Stevens lays bare what Dawne Shand choose to leave covered, and we get to see another side of the equation. However, uniquely among this collection, except perhaps for the issues raised by Leslie Haynsworth, she highlights the issues of working people and economic inequality in a significant way. Examples include the family's housekeeper in Jasper who sneaks behind their backs to use the washing machine and the people in Waverly whose water is poisoned with motor oil for an inability to pay the bill consistently. Like Ashley Day, Kyes Stevens brings up the matter of "good white people," that sarcastic euphemism, but she ends her memoir by asking who among us is perfect, with a blunt reckoning on the moral issues of the modern South: the situation is far from fair or just or perfect, and it is our duty to make it that way as best as we can. While she does see some changes in the South since the Civil Right movement, they are not nearly enough.

The next two memoirs in the collection explore very different sides of the city of Montgomery, but well after its days as an epicenter of Civil Rights activity. In her work, which is set in the mid-to late 1980s and early 1990s, Vallie Lynn Watson uses the metaphor of "Hiding Next Door" to raise issues of social class and how the upper echelons of "society" in Montgomery recycled old aristocratic ideas where friendships are fragile and the unacceptability of black people is assumed, not examined. Having moved to Montgomery as a teenager, Watson was involved immediately into the private school and country club culture that her parents, who were from Montgomery, were already familiar with. Watson took part in all of the "right" things, becoming a part of Montgomery "society," but somehow it seemed implicitly weak for her. The importance of Watson's memoir lay in the insider's view of an elite culture most Southerners only see from the outside and are not invited (or allowed) to attend. In this world, the social class aspect matters more than race, because race is a non-entity here.

Ravi Howard then, in "Elevator Music," keeps our focus in Montgomery during the same time period by looking at African-American life — another view that contrasts Watson's narrative — where the relics of an older black culture remained to remind that city's black population of a pride that seems lost but can still be regained. Howard's memoir utilizes the space, and certain locations, in Montgomery to build a memoir that analyzes the past, both his own and one that came before him. His thoughts harken back to the idea of standing on the shoulders of giants. However, he writes, "As those places fade, the sense of history within those walls becomes more distant." Howard acknowledges that the times have changed and are changing, and that, even though Montgomery is a place where history is people's real lives, the history and its meanings fade too as the people pass away and as the buildings and landmarks crumble. The importance of Ravi Howard's memoir adds another definite piece to the puzzle, as his clear pride in being African-American causes a distinct consciousness about race in a time when the racial tensions of the Civil Rights era were supposedly done.

The next-to-last work, by Ray Morton, brings us into squarely modern times. In "What Is There to Say?" Morton provides a necessary element in this broader discussion: that very real unknowing of growing up in acceptance, without conscious racial bias or a recognized confusion about it, but recognizing as an adult that it did exist. Morton was born in 1981, grew up in a suburb of Birmingham, Alabama, and attended public schools there. His narrative expresses the common idea among white

Southerners that racism is somehow both alive and well and a thing of the past at the same time, although Morton does question even his own behavior in a racially charged place. The memoir is something of a white conversion narrative, albeit one that Fred Hobson would dub less "exciting."

Once again, with all of these latter-day memoirs, I take exception with the necessity of excitement within a narrative to ensure its importance in the larger discussion. These more modern memoirs exist as recollections not altogether certain of the underlying ideas within their self-examinations. Watson's and Morton's memoirs falls roughly into the same category as the narratives in Hobson's *But Now I See*, for instance. These stories also evidence what scholar Eduardo Bonilla-Silva calls the "new racism" in his book *White Supremacy & Racism in the Post-Civil Rights Era*, which describes a subtler, less outwardly hostile attitude with more insidious, less recognizable manifestations. Where the demon to be exorcised used to be clear, the new demons have evolved into something that leaves room for questions: am I actually a racist? With the deeply disturbing connotations of being a "racist," this matter is difficult for many white people to resolve, or even explore. Debates continue today over the criteria of dubbing someone a racist: is it simply an attitudinal issue, or does a person have to have the means to enact a power struggle onto another person, thereby transforming the attitude into action?

As the final essay in *Children of the Changing South*, Kathleen Rooney's "Facing South" takes a look at her short time spent in the South, in Louisiana in the mid–1980s, with a father whose disdain for the region was open and apparent. She adds a different perspective to our long look at the experience of youth in the South — the comments of an outsider, someone who came to the South from another part of the country — and her story extends into her work on the groundbreaking presidential campaign of an African-American junior senator from Illinois.

David Molina closes out the collection with another unique perspective. Molina came from Ohio to the South, to Mississippi, as an adult, first to teach high school and later to work in the area of racial reconciliation. His Afterword explores two phenomenon: the "you ain't from around here?" attitude that Southerners are well known for, and the catharsis that occurs when people talk to one another about what lingers from the past. "Why is this collection of memoirs important and viable?," Molina asks rhetorically, and concludes that these discussions provide an opportunity to move toward greater understanding of how the South moved from its notorious past to its eminent present.

These memoirs, spanning a variety of Southern places and times, provide some hard looks back at growing up in the South in the 1950s, 1960s, 1970s and 1980s, and to being a child in the midst of very complicated events and social changes. These writers explore issues of not only race, but exponential issues of gender roles, social class, maturity, morality, language, apprehension, education, public policy, and job opportunities. As a child of this time period myself, most of the people my own age who I talk to seem to agree that we did our best to accept things as they were when we were children, and that we love our parents very much, but also that we have, as adults, questioned the facts of our upbringings very deeply.

Once the main era of Civil Rights Movement was done, once the 1970s and 1980s had come and gone, putting at least a full decade between a nation and the very public purgation of its most predominant ills, we have been left to recover, or to try to. It seems that it is my generations' job to attempt to pick up the pieces from the previous generations' battles. Some of the people who participated in or witnessed those battles impart the wisdom they gained when they can, although some others choose to remain conspicuously silent for their own private reasons. Those pieces of the past continue to lie around, waiting to be discovered again. I can remember my shock in 1995 when I read that the Mississippi state legislature had finally repealed the state law that made slavery legal; they had done this 132 years after the Emancipation Proclamation, 118 years after Reconstruction had ended, a full thirty-one years after the Civil Rights Act of 1964. Other matters were even more public *and* more personal, as in the re-openings of the 1955 Emmett Till murder case in 2004 and of the 1965 Jimmie Lee Jackson murder case in 2005.

Thankfully, works like the ones in this collection are now analyzing how the South can reconcile or recover or move on ... no one has quite decided yet what the South is to do next. One of my main intentions is for this book to be one of openness and hope, not another chronicle of how awful it once was. In my experiences working with Civil Rights commemoration and other projects that have involved race and Southern history, I have encountered people with deep wounds, strong opinions, justified anger, incurable resentment and fiery messages for anyone willing (or sometimes unwilling) to listen. I have volunteered to be secondhand witness to the immense pain that segregation, Jim Crow, and the Civil Rights Movement have caused to both black and white people, and I have worked when I could to be sure that memories are preserved as accurately as possible. However, what I always return to is the mantra that I hear at many events: "Look Back! March Forward!" The purpose of open dialogue about injustice in the South is not to pick the scabs, not to ensure that wounds fester, but to continue the legacy of the social justice movements of the mid-twentieth century, which were forces for positive change, for equality, for peace, and for freedom.

They say that time heals all wounds. Here we are, more than forty years after the death of Martin Luther King, Jr., the event that often marks the end of the Civil Rights Movement in many history books and textbooks. Here we are, into the first term of the first non-white U.S. President. (Whether any given person wants to label him as "black" or "mixed" ... I leave it up to them.) Time heals all wounds? We shall see.

Bibliography

Applebome, Peter. *Dixie Rising: How the South Is Shaping American Values, Politics and Culture*. New York: Random House, 1996. Print.

Ashmore, Susan Youngblood. *Carry It On: The War on Poverty and the Civil Rights Movement in Alabama, 1964–1972*. Athens: University of Georgia Press, 2008. Print.

Barnard, William D. *Dixiecrats and Democrats: Alabama Politics, 1942–1950*. Tuscaloosa: University of Alabama Press, 1974. Print.

Bartlett, Bruce. *Wrong on Race: The Democratic Party's Buried Past*. New York: Palgrave Macmillan, 2008. Print.

Bartley, Numan V. *The New South, 1945–1980: The Story of the South's Modernization*. Baton Rouge: Louisiana State University Press, 1995. Print.

_____, and Hugh D. Graham. *Southern Politics & the Second Reconstruction*. Baltimore: Johns Hopkins University Press, 1975. Print.

Blake, John. *Children of the Movement: The Sons and Daughters of Martin Luther King, Jr., Malcolm X, Elijah Muhammad, George Wallace, Andrew Young, Julian Bond, Stokely Carmichael, Bob Moses, James Chaney, Elaine Brown, and Others Reveal How the Civil Rights Movement Tested and Transformed Their Families*. Chicago: Lawrence Hill Books, 2004. Print

Cash, W. J. *The Mind of the South*. 1941. New York: Vintage, 1991. Print.

Dain, Martin J. "Porter L. Fortune Jr. History Symposium to Explore Childhood in the South." *Southern Register*. Center for the Study of Southern Culture. 22 Sep. 1995. Web. 12 Jan. 2011. <http://www.olemiss.edu/depts/south/register/95/summer/02histsy.html>.

Feldman, Glenn, ed. *Before Brown: Civil Rights and White Backlash in the Modern South*. Tuscaloosa: University of Alabama Press, 2004. Print

Fleming, Karl. "The South Revisited After a Momentous Decade." *Newsweek* (10 Aug. 1970). Rpt. in *Reporting Civil Rights, Part Two: American Journalism, 1963–1973*. 838–846. New York: Library of America, 2003. Print.

Hobson, Fred. *But Now I See: The White Southern Racial Conversion Narrative*. Baton Rouge: Louisiana State University Press, 1999. Print

_____. *Tell About the South: The Southern Rage to Explain*. Baton Rouge: Louisiana State University Press, 1983. Print.

Gaston, Paul. *The New South Creed: A Study in Southern Mythmaking*. Montgomery: NewSouth Books, 2002. Print.

Gladney, Margaret Rose. "Introduction to the 1994 Edition." *Killers of the Dream*. By Lillian Smith. New York: Norton, 1994.

Goldberg, Theo David, ed. *Multiculturalism: A Critical Reader*. Malden: Blackwell Publishers, 1994. Print.

Grobman, Laurie. *Multicultural Hybridity: Transforming American Literary Scholarship & Pedagogy*. Urbana: NCTE Books, 2007. Print.

Haskins, James. "The Humanistic Black Heritage of Alabama." *The Remembered Gate: Memoirs by Alabama Writers*. Eds. Jay Lamar and Jeanie Thompson. Tuscaloosa: University of Alabama Press, 2003. Print.

Jeffries, Hasan Kwame. *Bloody Lowndes: Civil Rights and Black Power in Alabama's Black Belt*. New York, New York University Press, 2009. Print.

Jones, Suzanne W., ed. *Growing Up in the South: An Anthology of Modern Southern Literature*. New York: Mentor, 1991. Print.

Kirby, Jack Temple. *Rural Worlds Lost: The American South, 1920–1960*. Baton Rouge, Louisiana State UP, 1986. Print.

Lee, Harper. *To Kill A Mockingbird*. 1960. New York: Warner Books, 1982.

O'Dell, Jack Hunter. "Notes on the Movement: Then, Now and Tomorrow." *Southern Exposure* 9.1 (Spring 1981). Rpt. in *Black Southern Writers*. Ed. John Oliver Killens and Jerry W. Ward, Jr. New York: Meridian, 1992. 442–451. Print.

Smith, Lillian. *Killers of the Dream*. 1961. New York: Norton, 1994.

Sokol, Jason. *There Goes My Everything: White Southerners in the Age of Civil Rights, 1945–1975*. New York: Vintage, 2006.

United States. US Dept. of Commerce. Bureau of the Census. *Household and Family Characteristics: March 1978*. 23 June 2010. Web. 11 Mar. 2011. <http://www.census.gov/population/socdemo/hh-fam/p20.../P20–340.pdf>.

Webb, Sheyann and Rachel West Nelson. *Selma, Lord, Selma: Girlhood Memories of the Civil Rights Days, as told to Frank Sikora*. Tuscaloosa, University of Alabama Press, 1980.

Power, Love and a
Sound Mind
by JACQUELINE WHEELOCK

By the time I learned to handle life's measuring spoon, I had already stirred up for myself a powerful fear-inducing opiate that largely controlled my every move. Its ingredients were what I perceived at the time as automatic strikes against me: blackness, femaleness, rurality, and being a Mississippian. While each ingredient eventually formed its own narrative, navigating and negotiating the blackness element took front and center during the sixties, as I found myself an impressionable teenager in the midst of the Civil Rights Movement.

Although still a largely overlooked fact, the inner responses of blacks to America's resistance to their enfranchisement are, at once, the same and totally different. My personal actions and reactions during and after the Movement dictated how I saw myself, as well as whom I was becoming. My story is a kaleidoscope of one Mississippi girl's fragile determination to make good on her country's promise and to mix for herself a fresh elixir, stimulating to the taste and good for the healing of the soul.

Love

Near Pascagoula, Mississippi, Summer 1958

What I remember most about that July day in the late fifties is the walk through the sandpit, the desert-feel of a merciless sun. Home was not far away now, just through the pit a little ways and up its south bank to the shade of live oaks, still harboring a few of last season's acorns in their root crannies. Mama would be waiting. Waiting to hear (without having to ask) what today's white lady paid, what she did not pay, what she did not say.

Soon after climbing out of the pit and stepping across the threshold into the cool dark kitchen, I felt the unasked questions coming from behind Mama's serene, though slightly palsied, mask: Did today's woman say thanks? Did she notice that you were a bright girl? Did she inquire about your grades?

"Not today, Mama," I answered wordlessly from behind my own mask. "The white lady only said, 'Be sure to move them mattresses.'"

The unasked questions continued: Did she give you a good lunch? Did she speak interesting things of her own life and children?

"No, Mama, not today. She only said — over and over, she said — 'Jest be sure you clean the winders and the walls.'"

Backing up to that morning before the sandpit walk, I recall the familiar novelty of the scene as the white lady's husband drove me into his yard. These were new white folks, but really not new at all, for I had been here before in my short life — on other roads on different mornings with the summer sun shining on other faded mailboxes bowing in submission to the timeless dirt roads. These were not the kind of white folks that offered steady work in air-conditioned houses. This was sporadic "day work" coming down from the working class, the class who drove up to our house in their Joad-like clunkers and announced to Mama, "Carrie Bell, my wife needs to 'use' one of your girls for a couple o' days next week." These were the ones who had to bite back "nigger" at every rise of their tongues and every turn of their minds, just to keep an uneasy peace while the work was being done.

But they were going to pay me $2.50 a day, and that was $2.50 more than I had. So when the new boss lady's husband drove up at 7:00 in the morning to pick me up for the first day of a two-day job, I knew to take my place as a colored girl — to crawl into the back seat of the car, itself seemingly condemned to a slow, tortuous death — and speak only when spoken to. But I also knew not to be surprised at the small weathered house staring at me, no larger than my own, set close to the constant swoosh! of the cars on Highway 63 into town.

The house was cool at 7:30, fans humming promises that I knew they could not keep against the daily relentless march of the Mississippi sun — nothing like the sweet controlled air of the gentry for whom I most often worked. But "that's okay," I thought. "$2.50 is $2.50, and I want to go to college one day." Subconsciously, I think I was being helped along by the images of unspeakable bravery I had glimpsed last year in girls who looked like me, walking toward a white fortress in Arkansas called Central High School so that they could be better educated and hopefully access any college they pleased. To this day, I don't know if Mama knew about the Little Rock Nine. We never spoke of it. The cusp of the Civil Rights Movement was otherworldly to me and my parents — wonderful and terrifying all at the same time. Still my dreams of succeeding were being fueled by the television and newspaper images. Every dime would help.

My boss lady for the day seemed somewhat ill at ease, but I was to discover soon that behind her unpolished effort to assume the role of the elite was a sure focus. She immediately started to drive me, not out of an innate meanness it seems to me in retrospection, but more out of a sense of desperation to make her self-perceived Queenness for Two Days count for all it was worth. Even through the misted eyes of adolescence, it was plain to me that her husband's living was not a wealthy one, probably not even a comfortable one from the looks of the cheap precarious iron bedsteads and the yellow pine furniture. And I imagine that her husband, out of a whimsical sense of nobility, had peeled off a ten and said, "Do what you want with it. Getcha some help like them rich beach women down in Pascagoula do all the time, if you've a mind to."

But I could stand being "used" for a couple of days. I had done day work before; I knew the look, the smell, the difference between the kitchens of the rich and the pantries of the poor, so I thought I knew what to expect.

Hardly ever looking at my face, my temporary white lady directed me to clean the windows and walls, a daunting day's work for an adult male, overwhelming for a young female who weighed less than a hundred pounds. And she instructed me to sun the mattresses. And sweep. And mop, and "while you're restin'," fold up the clothes. I think — at least, I choose to believe — she helped me with the mattresses.

By noon the motion of the fan's blades had been reduced to an annoying buzz, beating hopelessly at the hot air like stunned dragonflies. I was hungry. I was frightened. I wanted to go home, drink Kool-aid or go to the colored settlement's snack store and buy a six-cent Barq's Root Beer. In sum, I was still just a child.

Two o'clock came and I was still cleaning windows and walls. No mention of lunch that I can recall. Certainly, no mention of home. Three o'clock, more of the same. Then, under the sudden influence of a newly-kindled flame inside me of which I was not fully aware, I caught my boss away in some other room of the small house, and I struck out, without her permission and without pay, for the three-mile trip home.

There was a certain freedom for me in that scorching walk that was connected to the stone faces of the young black children that had integrated

Central High School in Little Rock. Though I had not the nerve to ask her to take me home when the time came, impulse and independence pushed me out of the house onto the hot, sandy shoulders of the asphalt. Then a turn east onto the side road leading to the colored settlement, and finally back south through acres of abandoned sandpit behind my father's property, no longer providing sand for dump trucks to expand the county highway system. I had never even heard of a sunstroke; thus any symptoms I might have had of heat exhaustion were overridden by my ignorance and determination to get to the shade of our yard. I figured I was in trouble. Deep-seated fear told me that, integration or no integration, one simply didn't do what I had just done: up and walk away from a white person's house without asking.

I must have been a heart-piercing sight to my mama when I entered the old house. As usual, she didn't ask her questions. She simply looked at my thirteen-year-old face slick with sweat, my recently pressed hair pulling back into its natural state, and said, "Supper'll be ready in a while. You can rest now." She asked nothing about why I walked home in the heat, said nothing about tomorrow. I assumed I would go again when the man came for me. Integration or no integration, I knew he would come. I was afraid.

Mama's unasked questions hung in the air beneath the low ceiling of our home all afternoon, but I was too young and too tired to think of anything else at the moment except being in the shade of that old unpainted clapboard house. Like many other similarities between our house and the lady's house from which I had escaped, we didn't have air-conditioning. But the dozen or so oaks always made sure that in our home the sun never took too much authority, never became too proud in its daily ascent.

Early the next morning I was lying half asleep in the front bedroom next to the porch, waiting for Mama to tell me it was time to get up and get ready for work, when I heard her voice from the porch speaking to the white man seated in his faded car.

"No, sir," she said in no uncertain terms, "she ain't goin' today. She won't be goin' back a'tall."

Mama's unasked questions of love and concern that always stood undying in her eyes, even as she sent me out to learn how to earn a living, remained between her and me throughout her lifetime. And even now, they cling to me like a freshly washed blanket. But her unspoken answer to the question that the white man must have wanted to ask that morning is far clearer to me today than it was in my thirteenth year:

"You want to 'use' one of my girls? Bring her back to me the way you took her."

A Sound Mind

Rochester, New York, Fall 1969

No matter where I went or what I accomplished, I hauled the baggage with me: infused fear, embedded inferiority, negative self-awareness all hidden beneath a mask of amiable confidence. By the fall of 1969, I was college educated and living in upstate New York — a foreign country. To my surprise, the Civil Rights Movement had touched not only Mississippi, but New York as well. My husband of four months had been accepted into a predominately white seminary in Rochester that had recently added a black church studies program. I became the default breadwinner, having quickly landed a job teaching at a junior high school.

Having spent the lion's share of the 1960s pursuing undergraduate and graduate degrees at a historically black college, I had so far missed the experience of intermingling with whites in professional settings. For the most part, people in authority on my new job were not only white, they were culturally different: simultaneously courteous and curt — offering none of the easy unhurried camaraderie I had come to expect among peers and inadvertently feeding my ever-present inferiority. On the first day of class when I looked at whom I was to instruct, an irrational fear gripped me. The children knew more than I did, I decided. After all, they were white *and* Northern. The repetitive words of a scratched record formed in my head: *I can't do this. I don't know enough. I haven't seen enough. I can't do this....* I never dreamed that first-time white teachers might have been hearing a similar tune. I got my first headache that day.

I quickly discovered that I had not had enough time to educate myself. I had read very little as a child, and during the blur of my higher education, I had been taught just enough to get started in the classroom, not nearly enough to get me through a whole year. Suddenly, I was faced with scores of idealistic, middle-class Northern children, and most of them were white. Every night, I drove myself to study and memorize the assigned lesson so that the following morning I could teach to my own mostly unrealistic, highly set standards.

I had always loved words, but there were countless words that had not been a part of the conversation in African-American rural Mississippi. If I heard a word pronounced — on "As the World Turns" or from the mouth of the mighty Cronkite — I quickly followed suit. But when I saw words in written form without the advantage of ever hearing someone use them (as I so often did), I made up my own pronunciations. I pronounced words as I saw them. In the fall of '69, "kaleidoscope" was a word I had not yet heard pronounced.

One morning while teaching a short story, I pronounced "kaleido-scope" as "kaLEEdoscope with a long "e" rather than a long "i." A white boy of about twelve years corrected me, the sound of the long "i" flowing from his lips as spontaneously, and perhaps as innocently, as the warble of a spring bird. It would seem that forty years later a minor happenstance such as that would have a vague place in my memory bank, overwhelmed by the wonderful school experiences that emerged in the days ahead. But that misstep in pronunciation is as vivid in my mind today as this morning's breakfast. Despite the re-created laws of the land, the Jim Crow stamp of fear and inferiority had indelibly been placed upon me, and the relatively insignificant error of a vowel sound sticks out to this day beyond all others events of my first year of teaching.

Following the child's correction, I didn't miss a beat as his instructor, but for the rest of the day, all the years of injected inferiority settled over me like a Biblical plague.

What in the world do you think you're doing? The charade is over. What ever made you think you could teach these children? You don't know enough. You haven't seen enough. You never will!

After a night of self-examination, I was right back in that classroom the next day. Though I was still lugging around the bottled fear and infe-riority and some perfectionist tendencies, I had added a trace of a new ingredient to my mixture, sound thinking: No matter what her race or place of origin, nobody on God's planet Earth knows everything. I would continue to self-educate for the rest of my life.

Atlanta, Georgia, 1974

Love

For the most part, each day I was wearing one of two maternity dresses recently purchased for me by a dear friend from church. One was blue, the other orange. Though I was eight months pregnant, fear of gunning my stick-shift Beetle across Atlanta via I-20 every day — its bright orange matching one of my two maternity dresses — was not an option. My hus-band was in a PhD program at Emory; we needed the money; and we had come too far to allow a minor thing like a daily struggle between steering wheel and swollen abdomen to stop us now.

Like the one in Rochester, the school where I was teaching just east of Atlanta was white in its population. But I had gained enough confidence in my work ethic to let a long sigh and shake of the head balm my ego when I made a mistake and move on toward doing what needed to be done in the interest of educating children.

The school system had been kind enough to hire me pregnant, fully aware that, come December, I would have to take maternity leave. The job went well from day one. I didn't know it at the time, but it was my love of literature that was making a name for me wherever I taught school, causing children who hated English to perch on the edge of their seats when we discussed a story. The teaching of literature transformed me into a fearless, focused vessel. The energy and love I put into it made me and the children forget what color I was and, in the case of my Atlanta classroom, how truly shapeless I had become beneath my orange and blue maternity dresses.

Days before it was time for me to take leave, I was about to take my tenth graders to lunch when they all struck out in front of me down the hall toward the cafeteria as though I had suddenly taken on an offensive smell. Tired and heavy with child, I made no effort to keep order that day. *They're good kids. I can trust them. They'll be all right.*

But when it was time to leave the lunch room, the same scenario occurred causing me to wonder if some of my conviction about their trustworthiness was misplaced. Again, I waddled a distance behind them back to my classroom.

When I passed through the door, a group of white parents, obviously infused with enthusiasm, had set up a wonderful surprise: a going-away celebration for me! The parents were warm, expressing how much their children liked my class. I was awash in humility and gratefulness to the children and their mothers. I had come a long ways toward ridding myself of the poison of fear.

The next morning, as I and my class took a moment to bask in the afterglow, one of the students whose mother had obviously worked hard to make the party a success offered a telling comment:

"Last night my mama said, 'I didn't know she was *black!*'" Meaning me.

The child laughed while I offered a half-hearted smile. Given where I had been fifteen years earlier as a black female in America, I couldn't help but be heartened by the fact that all those months I had taught a white child who never saw it important enough to mention my blackness to her parents. Love and respect had colorblinded the young girl.

But I wondered then — and I still do — if her mama would have participated so vigorously in the celebration of my teaching had she known I was black.

Lexington, Mississippi, 1975

Power

Few times have I ever been treated with overt cruelty by someone white. But when a sense of inferiority is catechized into you — when your mother, without saying a word, leads you to the back door to begin your first day as a domestic, when you know the unspoken rule of not sitting in the living room or not having dinner until their dinner is finished, then the fear of consequences if these lines are crossed is apt to follow.

I, along with my husband and children, moved back to Mississippi in early 1975, but this was another Mississippi from the one in which I had grown up. Unlike the coastal area in which I had been reared, this Mississippi was fraught with vestiges of cotton farming and plantation mentality. Words and phrases like "combines" and "cotton poison" were still very much a part of the local language, and a half-decade past the turbulence of the sixties, there remained a palpable tension between progress and stagnancy. On the one hand, the county to which we moved boasted, and rightly so, of the first black Mississippian to be elected to the state House of Representatives since Reconstruction. On the other, each month's beginning found Lexington's post office and grocery stores often strewn with manila envelopes — precious government income, signaling a troubling economic imbalance.

The town had a lovely old square — a concept unfamiliar to me as a coastal Mississippian — complete with an 1890s courthouse, long densely-packed apparel stores, furniture stores, and banks. Later on, access to such a graphically historic setting would remind me of Faulkner novels, but at the time, I was still quite young and had not self-educated enough to make the connection.

The extent of the repression that existed among the black population in this insular Mississippi town came clear to me on a spring-like day in the mid-seventies as I walked briskly toward a doctor's office. I had parked my car and was traveling on foot toward my destination. Admittedly, I have no recollection of my physical ailment, but I vividly remember that the front doors of the businesses sat almost on the sidewalk itself.

I suppose the lady coming toward me, whom I had never laid eyes upon in my life, sensed my body leaning in the direction of the doctor's front door. Had she known the inhibitions I had overcome to face that door, she might have relented. Instead, like a desperate mother watching her child about to walk in front of truck, the brown-skinned lady reached for me.

"No, no, no! Uh-umm, you can't go in there. You got to go 'round to the back. You can't go in that way. Black folks can't go in that way."

I guess I looked like a stranger to the town. Still, to her, I must have seemed some distant sister — some recalcitrant, uninformed youngster about to make one of life's dangerous irrevocable turns. The fear in her was trying to protect me; the fear in me recoiled into something close to anger — not toward my protectress, but toward the very personified Fear that already had me nervous, though determined, about what I was about to do. After all, it wasn't as though I didn't realize that blacks were still swimming upstream in the aftermath of hatred. Emmett Till had been killed. Medgar Evers had been killed. Malcolm X had been killed. Martin Luther King had been killed.

I could be killed.

"Watch me," I said, as I hastily withdrew from the woman's touch, turned the knob, and went through the door. To my knowledge I never saw her again. Had I seen her, I would have tried to explain my flippancy. I was as afraid as she was. The last thing I needed was fear on fear.

I doubt whether I was the first black person ever to enter that white waiting room as a patient, but it was clear that my presence in there was not the order of the day.

When I entered, the receptionist was businesslike if not pleasant — certainly not hostile. But the most disconcerting activity was on the other side of the receptionist's cubicle. I could hear what seemed like hordes of black people waiting to see the doctor. Memory suggests that I could even see some of them, but this is where memory and I are not in alignment.

Completely alone in that tiny waiting room, I felt as though I was trampling the toes of the Colossus. I expected anything; I expected nothing. But with the buzz of numerous black patients on the other side of the cubicle, the last thing I expected was to be waited on quickly. I rocked back and settled in for the long haul.

"Miz Wheelock, the doctor will see you now."

But what about the throng on the other side of the cubicle? Shouldn't they be first?

"Thank you," I said.

I smiled, picked up my purse and followed the nurse to an examining room. I was feeling a little powerful that day.

Covered Walkways

by Lean'tin Bracks

It was in 1964 when I witnessed the high school students of my hometown gathered on the football field with fear, and disbelief, on their faces, but mostly there were determined looks of possibilities and change. I wondered for a long time about their experiences and what would make them have such expressions. What had made the whole school come together for that moment, a moment, a necessary moment.

I was attending the junior high school then, which was across the street from the high school. I would often see the high school students coming and going, huddling together in groups at times, and alone and searching at other times. When school was out, this was the best time of all because there was football practice, and later band practice, which offered the sound and the movement that lit up the neighborhood and the community around the school. This was cool. Many a day, I stood in awe and anticipation, of the day when I would make the journey under the covered walkways of Woodland Junior High School across the street to the covered walkways of Lincoln High School. When that day came, I would cross into a world of grown folk, special looks, long deep sighs of infatuation, responsibility, determination, and recognition a world that had to be changed.

I grew up feeling safe and secure in a small black community on our side of the tracks. My parents, like most black parents, loved and nurtured their children and warned us about the white folk who would not see us, or see us only enough to dismiss us. My community was an all-black segregated part of town on the southeastern coast of Texas, and like most black communities, it was across the tracks from the white folks' side of town. Black doctors, black dentists, black teachers, and black principals were ever-present in our community. Black-owned stores, black-owned funeral parlors, black-owned taxi cabs, and black-owned hair salons were an investment, in our community by our community. And of course, the many churches that helped us deal with the world outside of our community. My church, Bell Zion Baptist, was right across the street from the high school. Funny, but on Sundays, I never confused the experiences. The school was always silent and reverent when Sunday came around. And the church was watchful and steadfast when school was in. We had several middle-class neighborhoods and my family lived in one of those neighborhoods. My dad was a school janitor and a hustler — in the good sense — and Mama was a teacher. My mama taught elementary school and believed that "no one was better than anyone else." I remember one time when my mother was informed by the school superintendent, who was white, that he was her superior. Mama immediately replied that he may be her boss but never, never, her superior. She almost lost her job that day. She said we would have had a tough time if she had been fired, but she knew "the Lord would make a way." Over the years her words have echoed in my ears. A sense of pride and self-worth came more from what she did as well as what she said.

During the 1960s, there were many moments when harsh realities invaded my world of childhood priorities and coming of age challenges. Oh yes, in the gym, school assembly, the bewildered looks of our teachers, people crying and speechless teachers with words just on the tips of their tongues. The trembling voice on the loud speaker announced that President Kennedy had been shot and killed! It was as though the air was sucked from the room. Sadness hung over the gym as each one of us waited for a parent to make it all okay. John Fitzgerald Kennedy was someone adults said "was on our side, but then, right is right." He was a good guy but nobody had warned me that this good guy was, to so many, the bad guy. No one had warned me that other people's hate could infiltrate my world and make me feel life's injustices so intensely. I soon found that the danger and panic on TV could reach through and invade my cartoons, my hopscotch and the trips around the corner to see my best friend Jackie.

While watching TV news coverage about the assassination of JFK ... I saw Lee Harvey Oswald get shot by Jack Ruby. As they were taking Oswald from one place to another, the news caster yelled that Oswald was shot, and I saw him fall. I saw it, but I did not see it — shock, awe, questions, audacity, disrespect, rednecks, white folks. When Martin Luther King, Jr., was killed, it was not that kind of news coverage, not so much moment by moment. Seeing King on the news was news, for black faces were not welcomed on the screen. News about us was not so much for us to know more, but to warn us to say less. But King, he spoke of change, fair play, the law — God's law. His words made us all get up and hope more, see more, do more! After his murder, the black folks, my folks, the grown folks were talking, and moving about, sometimes raising their voices, and sometimes speaking in low and controlled tones. I could not talk on the phone then because Mama's friends called and Daddy had somewhere special to go and something special to do. Others did their part as Robert Kennedy kept Memphis calm with his story of pain and James Brown lulled black folks to a low scream with his music of respect, pride and hope. And after Medgar Evers was murdered on June 13, 1963; after four little girls were murdered on September 15, 1963; after JFK was murdered on November 22, 1963; and later after Malcolm X was murdered on February 21, 1965, followed by King on April 4, 1968, the cycle of shock, fear, and despair became familiar, numbing, explosive. Neighbors, calls, Sunday service, organizations and talks over the back fence added to the news of *Jet* magazine, *Ebony* magazine, local black newspapers, organizations that told us what happened, but then I was 16, and protected. I remember moments that were emblazoned on my brain and heart, but not every moment. I was sad, and I could feel something was different, and changing, painfully.

When it came time for me to attend Lincoln High in 1966, I had the path of my brother and sister as trailblazers. Because our town — the black side — was small, everybody knew everybody so what I did or did not do, Mama and Dad got the scoop. *Extra! Extra! Guess what your little darling did?* I did not get into a lot of trouble, but I was sassy. I like that word, sassy; sweet and tart at the same time — that was me. My sister and brother were the best. My brother was the oldest and an honor student, which set the tone for my sister, who also was an honor student. He played in the band and my sister later became the band announcer.

After a few rounds of going to the office and being tart when I should have been sweet, I found my niche. School was okay. Assemblies were really something special, and I think we knew it at the time. I remember Julian Bond who came to our school, and I think Barbara Jordan came also. My gosh, she was so confident, and her English was so clear and precise, that she made me want to speak well so I could experience the respect and awe from others who might hear me speak. My mama was a stickler for speaking correctly; so much so, that we were accused of "sometimes" sounding like white folks. I don't think so. Considering the music in our lives, our culture, and the gift of song that we had as a family, it made sounding white, in my eyes, impossible! Rest assured, the church folks can attest to our gift of song, as my dad's Nat King Cole-smooth voice would be lifted in song on Sundays and the spirit would move us all.

Lincoln High was always alive with debate, sports, music, honor societies, and friendships in spite of the fact that white teachers had invaded. I only remember one teacher who did not seem to be interested in anything we did. She taught chemistry I think, but she left no impression other than the sound of the school bell when her class was over. Many of my other teachers were interested, kind, mindful of our futures, and cheerleaders for our doing our part in changing the world outside, which was coming more and more into the world of school. Practicing for fire-drills and hurricanes were standard practice for us since we were on the Gulf Coast, but a new drill was becoming an ongoing focus. Being a black kid who wanted to graduate from high school, to have opportunities and choices, to speak up and not shut up, to lead and not follow, and who saw justice as a right and not a privilege was becoming more and more of a dangerous thing.

I remember the first time the bomb-threat drill was sounded. The day started as usual. I walked to school with classmates from my neighborhood. My homeroom was always full of chatter as most of us had gone to school together for a long time. My first grade class, in elementary school looked a lot like my class in high school. Small towns mean you know everybody. After homeroom, I went to my first class, which was science. I was placed in a group of four and we were about to do an experiment when the bell rang. There had been several practice drills that told us what to do for the different situations. The sequence of sounds alerted us it was a bomb threat. The principal's voice came on the loud speaker and made his almost breathless announcement to follow the protocol we had practiced. There had been several practice drills that told us what to do for the different situations. The instructions to exit the school building as quickly as possible took on new meanings. As a freshman in high school, this was my first experience with a real bomb threat. We had been told to stay calm and quiet, follow our teachers and move swiftly to the exits. How do you stay calm and quiet when someone considers your life not worthy of continuing? Even though we had practiced what to do when the bell went off, the urgency and possibility of what could happen became quite real. Everyone was quiet, but definitely not calm. There were such feelings of tension in the classroom at that moment that a mere outburst would have sent us all into a frenzy.

As the class went out the door into the hallway, the students lead by the teachers, started moving down the long hallway toward the assigned exits. "Do unto others as you would have them do unto you." That is the saying my mama had on her second grade classroom bulletin board. From what I can tell, black folks have continually tried to play by the rules, but the rules are just not fair. As my class moved down the long hallway, we passed the exit to the auto shop where I often peeked in. The boy I had a crush on (who did not have one on me) was probably in shop class when the bell went off. We passed the room where I had biology class and successfully dissected a frog. I was going to be a nurse and assist my brother who was going to be a doctor. My English classroom was next, and I swore that the next time I went to class I would remember to be sweet and not tart. As we came closer to the exit that led to the outside, someone began to cry and it caught like a wave. Mortality had greeted us, and our youth seemed no longer without limits. But this lesson was to be realized another day. There was an audible sigh of relief, which could be heard as we stepped into the daylight. Once out of the main building we passed the band room and headed to the football field. We went as close as possible to the goal post farthest from the school building and turned around to face the school. And then we waited... I heard one of the teachers say that the caller, who for sure sounded white, said, "I'm gonna blow you ni*****s up."

If Klu Klux Klan–type people would blow up four little girls, then it was open season on us. If they blew up the school building, we would lose our school, our memories, our books, our education, and possibly our lives. Who would do such a thing? Do they hate us so much? Since Dr. King is gone, will Ralph Abernathy come? Will the police come to help us or hurt us?

The police arrived after a long while, and they came almost silently, for no sirens shattered the air to announce their urgency to help. A handful of mostly white men came to address a situation, which people from their side of town had created. I had seen on television how the police were unleashing their dogs on black folks and sometimes those people were my age. How truly different were these people? We did not feel safe then, but in truth more vulnerable. And we waited! In situations of danger, the mind forces us to find a means to protect oneself against the helplessness. A shout rang out against those faceless voices that terrorized us and tried to away our innocence. "This is just wrong! Cowards, cowards ... killers, murderers." And we stopped waiting!! We planned loudly to march and protest and shout and not take this terror!!! We must do our part to change things. Others were making a difference then so should we. We would prove ourselves worthy and not allow others around us to try and dismiss us. That day we had worked through the disbelief, the fear, and the anger toward a resolve. Growing up can come through experiences, but as a black child it often comes in moments. No more waiting.

As my classmates and I talked about our world and the world we were going to enter into, we knew we would have challenges. The things our parents, teachers, and preachers had taught us, showed us, and prayed about for us were clearer, and we understood the commitment. The faces of my friends were burned into my sensibilities, because I fully realized that tomorrow was not promised.

As the police cars began to leave and the teachers gave us the all-clear, someone asked, "Did they find a bomb?" Not *this* time! Somehow this warned us that today was a gift and not a promise. I never did go back into school that day as classes were cancelled. My mama came to pick me up and I saw her car in the line of parents coming to get their children. As I headed to the car, I saw the junior high school students watching us, the high school students, as we were moving about with very determined looks on our faces. The junior high students watched, not knowing the intensity of the lessons, they would come to know. They were where we had been and we knew that they had much to learn when it became their time to move from covered walkways to covered walkways.

There were many more bomb threats that followed after that day. After a while they became commonplace and by graduation the rumor was that one of our students had called in one of the last threats. Change can "sweep you up" or change can "knock you down," but change will not ... leave you untouched.

Black Bitch

by JIM GRIMSLEY

I turn in my desk to face Theona Bragg, look her in the eyes and say, "You black bitch." The sky outside is very clear, without a cloud, and through the tall, narrow-paned windows we can see the wide lawn in front of the elementary school and the playground where we will soon head for afternoon recess. I have been sitting in front of Theona for a couple of weeks, ever since sixth grade began the first week of September. She is one of three black girls in my class, assigned to our previously all-white elementary school under something called Freedom of Choice. No one has told me what this term means but I do not need to understand the legal idea behind it in order to understand that something enormous has shifted in the balance of the world, if Theona Bragg can sit in the desk behind mine at school. Always in the past, as far back as the beginning of time, white people and black people have been separated. Everyone says so, including Preacher John Roberts at the church and William Henry Potter who owns the Pure Oil Station on Main Street.

In school we are twenty-eight white and three black children aged eleven through thirteen, the oldest being Lon Larson, who flunked fifth grade and has been in our class ever since, and the youngest being me, with my late September birthday. We are the same class that, with the exception of Lon and Theona and the other two black girls, began school as frightened first-graders an eon ago and a floor below in Mrs. Nora Nell Larkhammer's first grade room, advancing in a body each year to a different classroom in the Alexander P. Normal Elementary School.

At some point over the last few days it has occurred to me to turn to Theona and call her a black bitch, those exact words. I have no idea who she is, other than that she is an intruder in my world, the quiet world of this elementary school class full of white children advancing neatly from one grade to the next. This is the only world that has any right to exist.

70

White people do not go to school with people like Theona. She belongs to the category called niggers by everybody in the whole wide world.

My only idea of people is that they must be white and I do not have any inkling that Theona is a person, too. No one has ever told me expressly that what looks like a dark-skinned human being is actually something other than a person, but the idea sits in my head quite plainly and I have never been presented with any reason to question it. My mother prefers that my sister, brothers, and I use the word, "niggra," however, because this word is considered to be more polite. A clean-spoken church woman like my mother finds the word, "nigger," to be too coarse, and the word, "Negro," to be faulty for other reasons that I will come to understand later.

The fact that my world is populated by creatures with this brown-to-black color of skin who fall short of human status is well ingrained in me by sixth grade. The neighborhoods where niggras lived are spaced between our white neighborhoods, but it is easy to consider them invisible, since they are places that can never have anything to do with me. The Heights is a neighborhood near Potter's Lake, and in Potter's Lake proper there is the Back Street, where niggras lives in a long street of houses, including a store, a pool hall, and a church. There is Murphytown where a lot of niggras named Murphy live, and they are all bricklayers and have built each other nice houses of brick. Out in the country a black family and a white family might have houses nearly side by side. The barriers that separate black from white are invisible but absolute, effective at any distance. But niggras did not live mixed into white communities in town, and white people did not move into Negro neighborhoods, wherever they might be.

Niggras are transparent, have made no impression on me that I can detect. I have learned to glide my gaze across their houses, to ignore their faces, to see nothing of their lives except what can be turned to comment. Because, for some reason, it is necessary, from time to time, for all white people to remind one another of the squalor and the degraded condition of the niggra.

This has something to do with my impulse to turn to Theona Bragg, to say the words to her, "You black bitch." I feel that she needs to be reminded who and what she is. She has come to sit in my world, in my classroom, with my people, which are the only people whose visibility makes any difference. She has asserted herself in a way that endangers my status, and I need to utter something that will let her know that I see right through her ruse. She might now sit in the second seat of the sixth grade classroom of Alexander P. Normal Elementary School but she herself is a niggra, a nigger. She is less than me and I need to let her know.

Throughout the afternoon I feel her presence in the seat behind me. The idea surfaces constantly, that Theona has forgotten she is a niggra and needs to be told. I am the one who should do it because I am brave and will say anything. I should turn to Theona and say, "You black bitch." Say it in this tone, linger on the vowels, and look her right in the eye. Show Theona I have no fear of her because I am superior. But I am without the need even for so much justification as that, without the need for any hesitation at all. With the certainty that Clarence Banks and Norbert Carlson will laugh, will think I am funny and brave. That Dolores and Jane and Vonabe will think I am outrageous.

Schools are for white people. I know that niggras go to school because on occasion, when we drive past the nearby J. W. Billie Elementary School, my daddy will say, "There's the nigger school." This is a fact that has to be pointed out every so often, in case one of us children might forget it.

The idea of the niggra is a large one, even though it has never been taught to me directly. The differences between white people and black people can be shifty in any particular case. The possibility always exists that a white person will slip and become niggrish. This can happen in various ways, and, often, only a person's neighbors are able to detect the change. Wearing too bright a color might be niggrish, especially in a man. For a woman to wear too much makeup was either niggrish or whorish, and either one was damnation. Clothes that are too tight or shoes that are too flashy are niggrish. Any oddity in a person's front yard might bear the taint. A white person who lets automobiles and appliances nest in the front yard is getting as bad as a nigger, in the eyes of anyone who cares to criticize. What anybody will tell you, though, to prove that he or she is not prejudiced, is that the worst kind of nigger is a white nigger, which is defined to be a white person who has become completely niggrish, who lives even worse than a nigger. White trash might as well be niggras, have all the bad habits, smell just as bad, cook dirty food, live in filthy houses, and thrive on squalor.

The taint of Theona, so close to me in her wooden desk, front butted to the back slats of mine, might easily reach me across the air and begin to darken me. Some form of this thought comes to me at the time. Not everyone is having to sit as near to one of the black girls as I am. There might be some implication to that.

Mr. Burrow, the teacher, deals with us as best he can. He is a sad old wrinkled man, with fleshy eyelids that droop in folds and a way of speaking that sounds as if his tongue is slightly too big for his mouth. I sit on the front row and can see the red veins in his eyes. Vonabe, who is his neighbor in Potter's Lake, claims she can hear his wife screaming at him to do the dishes in the evenings. I am braver than Mr. Burrow, but not so brave that I am planning to make my statement to Theona while he is in the room. I am sneaky and underhanded and I wait for Mr. Burrow to leave the room, which happens soon enough, due to his small bladder. He walks to the office or to the teacher's lounge. Maybe he has a call in the office from his wife, whom I have once seen standing behind the screen door of their house, a housecoat wrapped against her body, which is shapeless as far as I can tell, though there is a sharpness to her eyes that I can see from a distance, in the scant moments before she closes the door.

Our town, Potter's Lake, is too small to be called anything but tiny. There are about four hundred people living there, a place where a coastal road crosses a fair sized river, the Trent River, which is mostly known for joining with the Neuse River at Gibsonville. Theona lives in a house in Hatchville, a strip of houses near a crossroads where a lot of niggra families lived. I have seen her in her yard once when my mother was driving to Notnert for some reason, maybe to take one of us to get our shots from the Public Health Center. She is a large girl, outweighing me by pounds, with two fist-sized breasts flattened under her dress. Her skin is very dark, a brown-black without any hint of red, and her hair is short and nappy, worn in an uneven Afro. She has flared, full lips and a very loud voice. She wears simple cotton dresses that are a bit faded but not really much worse or different than the poorer white girls.

She has the fiercest eyes I have ever seen, full of a hot anger, points of hardness in the brown iris. Her presence behind me is so palpable it is as if she is pressing her hands against the flat of my back. I can feel her there constantly.

The moment is clear, sunny. The schoolroom has fifteen foot ceilings that seem, to me, impossibly high. Windows nearly reach to the top of the ceilings. An old-fashioned school building, Alexander P. Normal Elementary School is named after its most famous principal, whose daughters, the Normal sisters, still live in a big white ramshackle house that sits back from Main Street behind a deep lawn dotted with trees. One of his daughters is the second grade teacher at the school and the other is the secretary. They both have skin as white as powder, crepe-soft and pin-wrinkled, quivering as they move their heads.

I turn to Theona, and a moment of silence happens into which I say the words I have been planning. The moment has come. "You black bitch," I say, and Lon and Darnell look at me and grin.

"You white cracker bitch," she says back to me, without hesitation, and cocks an eyebrow and clamps her jaw together.

I blink.

"You didn't think I'd say that, did you?" Her voice is even louder than usual, and her eyes flash with some kind of angry light. Everybody is listening. "Black is beautiful. I love my black skin. What do you think about that?"

"You are a black bitch," I say again, stupidly, and even though Mark and Norbert are snickering and I can tell they think I am really brave, I feel a little queasy.

"And you a white one," she says again and folds her arms across her breasts.

Pretty soon after that Mr. Burrow returns. Theona never says a word about what I have called her. All the rest of the day, I can feel her gaze boring into my back.

She has reacted to my declaration in an unexpected way. When I call her that name, she is supposed to do something else, she is supposed to duck her head or cringe or admit that I am right, that she has no business being in our white classroom. But she has taken what I said very calmly and has looked me in the eye and returned me word for word. In her sharp eyes and loud voice are evidence of a spirit tough as flint, a person unlike any of the milder beings around me.

She has a voice so big it pushes me back into my desk. To make such a big sound come out of herself causes her no fear. I can sing loud in the choir but otherwise I have a quiet voice. She is very different.

The next time she catches me looking at her, she says, "What you looking at?"

"You," I say.

"You got anything else to say to me?"

"No."

"Because I'm black and I'm proud of it." Her head is moving as she speaks.

"Say it loud," Vonna Cooperton said.

"I'm proud of my skin color. At least I ain't speckled up like you are."

I have a crop of freckles from summer sun, and blush under them.

"He blushing," Isafina Cooperton says.

"He cheap," Vonna agrees. "Look at him. He cheap now."

The three girls are like a chorus, their heads moving, their voices bold and big, sitting up straight in their desks.

This is a few weeks into the school term. The first few days my white classmates and I mostly ignored the black girls. They sat in their desks with stony looks on their faces and ignored us, too. Nobody said a word about the change, but there they were, every day, climbing onto the school bus out of the driveway of their neat brick home and coming to our school just like we did.

We ignored them and then somebody said something about one of them to make the rest of us giggle, and then I get brave and say my three words and Theona makes me cheap and Mr. Burrow comes back.

To make a person cheap, you spar with that person verbally till one of you achieves a good insult over the other. You win the game by how clever you are, or how loud you are, or how confused your opponent gets. You win the game with timing. In the case of the contest into which I have stumbled with Theona, I lose on the latter two counts. She gets loud and I stammer and blush. She wins on the count of timing as well. There I am, cheap until I can redeem myself, and publicly defeated.

Cheap is a game that the black girls bring to Alexander P. Normal. We white kids have never used the word in that way. But it is easy to understand, especially when I have just demonstrated it so clearly.

The next day I turn to Theona and she looks at me with her eyes piercing and ready and asks, "You going to call me any black bitch again?"

"No."

She raises her voice and made sure everybody could hear. "You better not."

That little move of her head, why does it fill me with the feeling of difference? Do the other white kids see this the way I do?

She is real. Her voice is big and it reaches into me. Her skin is a color I have never studied in any detail, a chocolate brown, clear and soft. Her lips are big and flaring. White people make fun of black people's lips. But Theona hardly seems self-conscious about hers.

If I am superior to her, why doesn't she feel it, too?

I call Theona a black bitch, but I never call her a nigger. Why do I stop short of that word, when what I want is to humiliate her? What has she already taught me, simply through her presence in the desk, breathing and speaking and looking around? Some part of me has already recognized that it was wrong to call her a nigger, that the idea is wrong. Some part of me has already seen there was not much difference between Theona and me.

Conversion

by LILLIE ANNE BROWN

My eleventh-grade history teacher, Mrs. Byrd, was a heavy-set, eccentric white woman who sat atop a too-small stool in front of the class and lectured from an ever-present textbook whose shiny cover depicted the image of a huge United States flag waving in the breeze. She spoke in a Southern drawl and peered over brown-rimmed glasses every few seconds as she looked up from the pages from which she frequently read. She always held a yellow sharpened pencil in one hand, though she never made notes on the pages of her text, which she held onto firmly as if any sudden movement would cause the book to slip from her grasp. Her short, fiery red hair, tufted over the ears, made her appear flight-ready from the classroom at a moment's notice. In a room of nearly all-black students, her nervousness was more than apparent. She always seemed one doorknob-twist away from a hasty exit. *Too much, too soon, too many*, she seemed to be thinking.

I wasn't quite sure how the history class came to be nearly all-black. In 1969, the third year of public school integration in Tallahassee, I believed there should have been a more diverse student population. There were a few white students who huddled near the edge of the classroom, but they were clearly outnumbered. And eerily quiet. I thought perhaps the black students had been so greatly lumped together because such a group could be more easily contained if racial unrest occurred on the sprawling campus. After all, black students and white students in the city were still pretty new to this whole school integration thing, so anything was possible. Black students had been bused to predominantly white schools in droves over the past three years in an effort to achieve some sort of district-wide racial equalization.

There had been no public counseling sessions, leadership conferences, or intervention seminars held in the community to help students to transition to new academic environments. If such sessions occurred, they were conducted primarily in the privacy of students' homes by parents of the students who were making the ultimate sacrifice of moving from one's school in their respective district to another school located several miles from their homes and neighborhoods. Parents' words of confidence and encouragement were the most beneficial. Children and parents across the city were paying close attention to the "content of their character and not by the color of their skin" and the "little black girls and little black boys" passages in the Reverend Martin Luther King, Jr.'s 1963 *I Have a Dream* speech. As much as the churches could, they, too, tried to prepare students for "the change." The themes of many Sunday sermons centered around the racial changes taking place in the South.

For many black children facing the unknown, Reverend King's speech had great relevance to our positions in new academic locations, and his words rang mightily in our consciousness. The mandate to integrate had been made, after all, by wise officials at the district office who felt that parity could *only* be achieved if black students made the sacrifices and embraced change. No one else, it seemed, needed to make such transitions in the name of equality. Ultimate adaptation seemed the primary goal.

No matter what chapter, topic or subject Mrs. Byrd informed the class she would cover during subsequent weeks during each academic period of the school year, she was determined to stick to her pre-ordained script of reminding everyone of the significance of Abraham Lincoln's "most notable deed" as the nation's sixteenth president. Week in and week out, the history lessons always made their way back to Lincoln's "magnanimous act in freeing the slaves," as she so often phrased it. The text was, of course, filled with great nuggets of historical significance, and oftentimes she would try to disguise the perch-stool lectures by inserting tidbits of information unrelated to slavery. But the ruse, worn, trite, and exhaustive, was always overshadowed by the subsequent return to, as she so proudly proclaimed, "Mr. Lincoln's greatest presidential act." She sometimes appeared weary of her own exhortations on the subject, however, and leaned slightly toward other historical and intellectual impulses. In the end her compulsions always gave way to the decisive topic of choice, and she would acquiesce without hesitancy, consideration, or further deliberation.

During the rare occasion when she thought to introduce a new topic, she would pull a three-sixty in the midst of her stream-of-consciousness discourse and backtrack to Lincoln & Co. as if she suddenly remembered where she was and who sat before her. Surely, she seemed to reason, there was no need to discuss any other topic of historical relevance: *What can be more enlightening*, I imagined her saying, *than acknowledging the signifi-*

cance of being free and paying homage to the man responsible for all liberties?
I'm being quite the gracious one here by bringing forth this vital information.
Can you all show just a little appreciation?

She seemed a little perplexed and quite perturbed at times that students did not parallel the enthusiasm of her oft-repeated subject. Student-reciprocation came in the form of apathetic stares as she talked non-stop and spoke with sheer reverence about "that great deed." Sitting in the second row of seats near the front of the classroom, I visualized her wearing a Confederate hat and dressed in the traditional uniform of a Confederate soldier. In an effort to drive home her point, I clearly expected her to appear in class one day with parched scroll and bayonet in tow.

I rarely listened to her lectures and failed to respond to the numerous interrogations and inquisitions to the class on any topic related to slavery, Lincoln & Co., and how each, as she insisted on repeating, "could not function without the other." I cringed at every syllable she uttered and quietly seethed. The period of newly integrated schools was a time of civil unrest and demonstrations across the South. If she wanted to, I determined, she could bridge the past with the present and get a real dialogue going on with the students. I suspect that we all would have been receptive to such a discussion, that we would not be opposed to such an undertaking. In fact, we would gladly welcome any diversion from the current lectures. For Mrs. Byrd to divert, however, would constitute a breach of her own biases, and she would not be part of any such discussions or succumb to any imagined interest from students.

I was a budding student of literary protest writings, slowly coming into my own as a reader of what I termed "high-end" literary works. I had been reading works by Richard Wright and James Baldwin for a few years, and I was seriously stumbling through Eldridge Cleaver's *Soul on Ice* and W. E. B. Dubois' *The Souls of Black Folk*. I tried deciphering Franz Fanon's *Wretched of the Earth,* but immediately recognized that I needed to put the work away and return to it after a more mature understanding of the writer's argument. I knew early on that background shaped the writer's art, but Fanon's "art" was, at the time of my reading, quite out of my league. I knew my limitations.

I had become interested in autobiographical writings as well and revisited, for the third time since age ten, Ethel Waters' *His Eye Is on the Sparrow*. I stumbled upon a copy of Claude Brown's 1965 tome, *Manchild in the Promised Land*, shared the work with a friend, and the two of us subsequently engaged lively discussions about the author's youthful days spent in Harlem, New York. I read as many books as I could get my hands on —

works that spoke to my experience and words that spoke to me — and I sought books by black women writers in particular. I spent lunch periods in the school library in search of books that didn't reference Abraham Lincoln or his magnanimous presidential deed. The lectures that Mrs. Byrd gave in class nearly every day were part of the historical legacy of black people in the South, but they were not part of my present-day experiences. I wasn't anti–Lincoln or anti-lecture. I simply needed more that was being offered at the time.

Very early during the time spent in her class, I had devised a way to combat my youthful literary angst while conforming to the ambience of the classroom setting. I decided that I would secretly read my own books during her sermons from the mount. The action, I concluded, would serve as a temporary respite from the mind-numbing lectures. Dual objectives would most certainly be met: Not only would I be present and accounted-for, I would also be engaging a private, literary performance for an audience of one. When I surreptitiously tuned her out and directed my attention instead to my own private agenda, I immediately lost myself in dialogue, descriptions, characters, and cultural connections that called my name and beckoned me to the pages. I became one with many of the authors whose works I read, voices I heard, and experiences I could relate to.

On the rare occasion that she caught me reading in class — and thus not giving her due propers — she made sure that I recognized her displeasure, once telling me after class, after she had spotted me reading Wright's *Black Boy*, that I needed to "put all that stuff away and listen to me." Her stern upbraiding became the fuel I needed to continue my literary enterprise in her class, and I engaged the endeavor a bit more stealthily. I suspected, however, that she knew, but I surmised, also, that she did not wish to say any more to me than was absolutely necessary. We were, after all, dancing to different drummers.

At the end of the year, she asked to write in my yearbook. I thought the request a rather odd one, especially coming from a woman who barely knew the names of her students, appeared fearful of turning her back to the class to write on the blackboard, and who was obviously disinterested in anything outside the realm of the "great document of 1863." But I handed over the book, curious to know what insightful comment she might wish to share. She had not, to my knowledge, made this request of any other students in the class. When I read the inscription, upon leaving the classroom for the last time, however, I can't say that I was shocked, surprised, stunned or enlightened by the words she wrote. She was, after all, the lady in charge, the one who had called the shots for a solid year, the one whose lessons never wavered from one day to the next. Maybe, I surmised, she wanted to offer some academic tidbit of support on the importance of expanding my literary repertoire, or perhaps she wanted to direct me to other scholarly sources that she felt would interest me. I was, after all, sixteen years old and quite idealistic. What she had boldly scrawled across a back page of the yearbook, however, was none of what I had envisioned. She had penned a clear and compact version of her year-long lecture to the class, directed specifically to me: "I'm sorry, Anne, that I wasn't able to convert you."

What Mrs. Byrd meant, I surmised at the exact moment of reading her words, is that she wished that I had been more accommodating and less on the verge of what she believed was an aesthetic militancy. Her appeal was for me to be more appreciative of and receptive to her daily lectures on slavery and graciousness. I needed, in her frame of consciousness, to be more accepting of her willingness to "educate" me, and I certainly needed to show a bit of gratitude regarding black folks' freedom in a country that, in her words, "didn't allow Negro children to even go to school with the Whites until now."

I concluded very early in the class that Mrs. Byrd was caught in a time capsule, unable to extract herself psychologically from the vestiges of segregation or the historical impact of "Lincoln's act." Her verbal onslaughts in class, coupled with the written words in my yearbook, conveyed the message that I, a young black girl with an interest in words and experiences that spoke to me, shouldn't have a desire to read or indeed an inherent need to know anything other than what she believed I had a need — and thus a right — to know. Though it was springtime, the imaginary ice beneath Mrs. Byrd's feet began a rapid melt.

I read the inscription on the way to my next class, but I felt an immediate urge to return to her classroom. My face stung with indignation. She needed, I concluded, to engage a full and proper accounting of her comment. She needed to know — and she needed to know from me — that her sense of propriety, authority, and vanity was certainly without merit. Or jurisdiction. She needed to know that her primary obligation was to teach and to do so without bias or interjection of personal proclamations that showed favoritism toward an ideal, theory or argument. In my brisk and determined walk to her classroom, I had mustered up an unknown energy. I wanted her to know that she, not I, was a prime candidate for so-called "converting," but as I approached her classroom, I saw that she had closed the door and had no doubt begun readying the stage for her next audience of idealists.

Growing Up Out of Place

by Becky McLaughlin

I was recently commiserating with a friend about what it means to be a Southerner, and she said she'd never quite been able to articulate the vague sense of worry and guilt she had grown up with as a descendent of General Robert E. Lee — until she read Lillian Smith's *Killers of the Dream*. For her, the book was a kind of godsend, and so she loaned it to me, thinking it would be the same for me. Her enthusiasm for the book compelled me to begin reading it right away, but within the first few pages, I realized that it was not going to do for me what it had done for her. And so I put the book down in disappointment, not because I thought Smith had nothing important to say, not because I thought Smith was lacking the earnestness and elegance that I expect from personal narrative, but because the experience she describes is one with which I am unfamiliar. Although Smith and I both identify as Southerners, she writes as someone who is very much in place, while I am someone who has always felt out of place. For better or worse, Smith belonged to a group that she could call "[her] southern people"; she evinces a strong sense of possession and belonging that I have never been able to achieve. Why were our experiences so different?

The answer is that what Lillian Smith learned growing up is pretty much the opposite of what I did. She wrote in *Killers of the Dream*:

> I learned it is possible to be a Christian and a white southerner simultaneously; to be a gentlewoman and an arrogant callous creature in the same moment; to pray at night and ride a Jim Crow car the next morning and to feel comfortable in doing both. I learned to believe in freedom, to glow when the word *democracy* was used, and to practice slavery from morning to night. I learned it the way all of my southern people learn it: by closing door after door until one's mind and heart and conscience are blocked off from each other and from reality [29].

While it's true that I, too, grew up in the South *and* in the Christian church, it is not true that I was taught to close doors that shut mind, heart, and conscience off from one another and reality. Instead, I was taught that the kinds of contradictions Smith mentions in the passage above are what stymie any chance we have of being true followers of Jesus Christ, any chance we have of moving a little farther away from being a racist society, any chance we have of not living out our lives in utter hypocrisy.

The year was 1957, and my parents were living in Los Angeles, my father attending flight school and my mother working as a telephone operator. They were both young, absconded Southerners. My father was 22, a Methodist farm boy from the hills of North Carolina; my mother was 18, a small town Pentecostal girl from the flatlands of southeastern Missouri. Once during their courtship, my mother came to pick up my father for lunch, and she saw a handsome, young black man standing close by. She said to her new white beau, "That colored man is nice looking ... for a colored man," to which her beau replied, "Any decent Southern boy would slap you silly for that remark." My father didn't slap her silly; he didn't slap her at all; so we only can surmise that he was already incapable of living up to the standards of what a "decent southern boy" would do, a felicitous failing on his part, one that would later pave the way to a complete collapse of the "decent southern boy" paradigm for him.

Perhaps in the 1950s all of the United States was "Southern" or, as we have come to understand the term — "racist." Just two years earlier in a 1955 address given by Perry Miller, a professor of American literature at Harvard, we find him arguing that only Negroes and Indians "can do things by instinct" (5). "Maybe," he continues, "that is why Willie Mays is the greatest of contemporary outfielders" (5). Maybe that is why the Indians "could never construct an assembly line or work out a split-second television schedule" (5).

These were the Fifties, and no doubt comments like my father's and Perry Miller's were being made all across the country, but the thing I find interesting about these comments and the reason I juxtapose them is this: whereas Miller could say what he said with a casual lack of awareness concerning the racist nature of his statement, my father was already aware of a problem or a split in his consciousness. Miller describes a "complex fate" in his address that was and is even more complex for the Southerner than for the Northerner. Miller could say what he said because, as a Northerner, he did not perceive himself to be "always already" guilty as his Southern sisters and brothers did. If I cannot relate to Lillian Smith's narrative, I'm betting that this would not be true for my parents because they were becoming adults — enlightened adults — during the Civil Rights Movement, and I benefited from having grown up in the aftermath of their enlightenment.

My parents married in June of 1958, and by August of 1959, they were back in North Carolina, where I was born. The following year, they moved to Memphis, where my father put his flight training to use as a crop-duster in the cotton, rice, and soybean fields of the Mississippi Delta. My sister Bonzie was born in 1960, the same year Elvis returned from his brief stint in the Army. In 1961, our little nuclear family moved from Memphis to a small town in southeastern Arkansas named Stuttgart, which still prides itself on being "the rice and duck capital of the world." It was the perfect place for my father to build his reputation as a crop-duster.

Although Stuttgart was smack-dab in the middle of Delta Blues country, I didn't know anything about the lives and music, or even the existence, of black people because in 1961 integration had not yet occurred in this small town. The blacks quite literally lived on the other side of the railroad tracks that split the town in half. And so even though my mother tells me that a black woman named Leda Madlock used to clean house for us once a week, I have no recollection of her. I have combed my memory for a trace of her face or voice, but there is a blank in the spot where she should be. I could explain this scotoma by saying that between the ages of two and four, I was simply too young to have begun creating vivid memories — and in part this would be true, for when I think back to that small house on Leslie Street, the colors are pale and washed out — but the real truth is that I simply had no system of intelligibility in place for understanding Leda Madlock's presence in our home. The categories of organization that give shape and value to what we see and hear did not include, for me, our black cleaning woman. "White" was an absolute term, the only one that had meaning, and because the categories by which we organize the world shape seeing itself, I could not "see" Leda Madlock.

However, there were things I did see, and they were frightening. It was a difficult time for my parents — those early years in Stuttgart — because my young father was absorbed in his work as a pilot, and my still younger mother was already responsible for a household and two small children. She was barely old enough to vote or buy booze, but she had already taken on a job that requires more creativity, patience, skill, and thought than any other job on earth: parenting. And so there was a good deal of fighting, as would be the case in any fledgling marriage, especially when the two partners are so wretchedly inexperienced. No doubt, it was desperation but also hope that led my parents to First Presbyterian Church, which sat on the corner of Maple and Seventh Streets, and to a long-lasting friendship with the minister and his wife, John and Ellen Goode.

When my parents speak of those early days in the church, they explicitly use the phrase "conversion experience" to describe the transformation that occurred in their marital and spiritual lives. They didn't speak in tongues, see the face of God in a stain on the side of a house, or have stigmata supernaturally impressed upon their bodies, but they might as well have. Like Paul on the road to Damascus, my parents had a miraculous, revelatory vision (or, perhaps more accurately, a *re*vision), which turned an apocalyptic God full of wrath into a loving and forgiving God. This new vision led, as it did for the Apostle Paul, to their becoming missionaries — not the kind who convert non–Christians to Christianity but the kind who wish to be of service to fellow human beings in need. If the Presbyterian church is best known for its doctrine of predestination, my parents injected a healthy dose of what I would call Sartrean existentialism into their faith, believing as Sartre does that existence precedes essence: that what we do in and with our lives shapes who we become and that if we observe wrongs in the world and do nothing to right them, we become complicit in continuing those wrongs. So when the Presbyterian Mission Board contacted my father in 1964 to ask whether he'd be willing to go to the Belgian Congo as a bush pilot, he and my mother agreed to take their family out of the Mississippi Delta and into the heart of Africa — an incredibly gutsy decision on the part of my parents, given their youth and inexperience, but one born of true Christian zeal.

It was in the Belgian Congo that I came to understand the concept of difference, came to understand that, here, we were the different ones, for when Bonzie and I accompanied my father on his flights into the bush to deliver medicine or doctors, the entire village would turn out to meet us. Descending out of the sky and then standing in the shadow of the airplane wing, Bonzie and I must have appeared quite alien to the Congolese children. Perhaps we were now in Leda Madlock's position — beings whose reality could not be registered simply through sight but through the visual coupled with the haptic, and so a curious child would often dart out of the assembled crowd to feel our hair, Bonzie's bleached white and mine golden by the hot African sun. Understanding the concept of difference meant that I ceased to be colorblind — that is, blind to skin color other than white — for given that our white family was very much in the minority, the color black could no longer be ignored. Of necessity, it had to be registered. And thus "white" was no longer an absolute term but a relative one; and my memories were no longer pale and washed out but aglow with the colors of Africa: the rich orange-red of palm nut oil, the lush green and pink of the Mimosa tree, the vibrant purple of the small flowers Babbalusamba wore in her ears, the chocolate browns and lemon yellows of the fabric in which the Congolese women wrapped their bodies.

It was also in the Belgian Congo that I intuited, in the fuzzy way children do before they have all the concepts they need for verbal articulation, a truth people (especially politicians) like to keep covered up: that one of the best tactics for maintaining the polarization of "us" versus "them" is to demonize "them" not as individuals but as a group. My experience in the Belgian Congo showed me, however, that one cannot tag an entire population of people "good" and another "bad" (to use the simplistic terms of children and some adults, for in any group there will always be some of both). For example, the Congolese man who washed and ironed our clothes and generally functioned as housekeeper for our family — his name was Gilbert, but it was pronounced "zhee-bear"— always welcomed my sister and me to share his evening meal. He lived in a one-room shack with a dirt floor, and his meal was a simple one: *bedia* (a dough-like substance made of manioc flower mixed with water) dipped in palm nut oil and, if he were lucky, the occasional piece of meat or mess of greens. He also functioned as a kind of makeshift doctor for our family, instructing my mother to plunge my hand into a bucket of kerosene when I had badly cut my finger, and digging a jigger out of my sister's toe with the bottom end of matchstick to prevent rupturing the egg sac. The military police, on the other hand, were very scary, and they seemed to revel in their ability to intimidate. So here were examples of the "good" and the "bad" co-existing side-by-side in one group of people.

I was eight when we returned to the States in 1967; the Vietnam War was at its peak; Richard Nixon was running for president; and our family was in Arkansas again — this time in Little Rock. At first, we lived on Oak Park Drive in a white suburb, where my sister Bonzie and I attended an all-white school. (Appropriately enough, my teacher's name was Mr. White.) I still carry with me a dime-sized scar on my knee that is slightly whiter than the skin surrounding it — the result of being knocked down on the playground and hurt so badly that the nurse sent me home to recover. Although the boy who slammed into me as he was playing chase did so unintentionally, the wound, gotten on the first day of school, came to symbolize a number of things: the insular, white experience in the aftermath of Africa, being knocked off balance by our return, the pain of contact with something bigger and more formidable than I, and the growing sense that I would never be "in place" again, that I would always be marked an "outsider."

The years in Africa had made it impossible for my parents to feel comfortable in an all-white community, and so the following year, 1968, we moved into a "changing" neighborhood in downtown Little Rock and joined an interracial church, Central Presbyterian. Just as we had arrived in the Belgian Congo during the exodus of the colonizing Belgians, we arrived in downtown Little Rock during the exodus of whites to the suburbs. So once again we found ourselves in the minority. Although I didn't know it at the time, Central Presbyterian had played an important role in the Central High School crisis. In Roy Reed's book *Faubus* about Arkansas governor Orval Faubus, he writes, "A few white ministers risked their positions by preaching that segregation was immoral" (238), and the Rev. Dunbar Ogden, pastor of Central Presbyterian, was one of them. Because he spoke up for integration, he lost his pastorate and, in 1960, his son David committed suicide "because of a depression that his friends traced back to the Little Rock crisis and to a campaign of harassment against him by segregationists and by friends who considered him a traitor" (239). How fitting that in the years following David Ogden's death, the church itself became integrated.

Living in downtown Little Rock was mostly a positive experience. We loved our two-story house with its architectural eccentricities and its backyard full of pecan trees; we loved our church and its minister, Bill Twitchell, with whom my parents became fast friends; and we loved our newly-adopted baby brother, a three-month-old Hopi Indian from Phoenix, Arizona. Bonzie and I did not, however, love our school. Parham Elementary, which sat in a black neighborhood, was integrated, but it wasn't a welcoming place. There was something sullen and unforgiving even in its physical structure, and, worse still, was my fourth-grade teacher, whose name was Mrs. Merry but whose pedagogical approach was anything but that. Looking back on it now, I wonder if her hostility toward me and my classmates had to do with the fact that she was a white teacher forced by circumstances to teach in what had been a black school. The only relief I had from Mrs. Merry were the moments spent on the playground in the company of a black fourth-grader named Victoria, the sole friend I made that year. Although my memory of Victoria is foggy, I do recall that she wore purple ribbons in her hair, and so I've since had a fondness for the letter "V" and the color purple.

It may sound as if we had managed to stamp racism out of our lives, but racism is an insidious thing, and there are pockets of it in the most unlikely places. This was probably one of the hardest lessons I had to learn — one I'm still digesting — and I learned it at the expense of my sister.

One morning before school, the telephone rang, and when Bonzie answered it, she heard Bill Twitchell's cheerful voice on the other end. He was calling about carpooling arrangements since his son attended the same school Bonzie and I did.

"Is it my turn to take you kids to school or your mom's?" he asked.

"I don't know," said Bonzie.

"I don't know, either," said Bill.

Being an eight-year-old, it occurred to Bonzie to resolve the issue with an old jingle, which she began to recite in her sweet, childish, singsong voice.

"Eeenie-meanie-minie-mo, catch a nigger by the —"

And there it was, hanging in the air between them — what has come to be referred to as the "N-word," a word banished (and rightly so) from everyday white vernacular for the rest of the foreseeable future. Bonzie dropped the telephone receiver and began to cry hot tears of sorrow and bewilderment. Where had that word come from? She had never said it before and would never say it again, but in that one moment it had welled up from some buried part of the collective unconscious. She didn't want to go to school that day or face Bill Twitchell because of the shame she felt for what she had said. I can't help thinking that the horror of this accidental utterance is what led her, in later years, to volunteer with ACORN and then to become a partner at Koinonia Farm, the interracial community near Americus, Georgia, started by Southern Baptist minister Clarence Jordan and his wife, Florence, in 1942.

In 1969, when I was ten, we moved back to rural southeastern Arkansas, not far from Stuttgart, because my father had been asked to become partners in a crop-dusting outfit called Grand Prairie Flying Service. It was a difficult move for my mother — she didn't want to leave Little Rock, didn't want to return to a narrow-minded, backwater town like the one she'd fled when she moved out to California — but it was an important business opportunity for my father, and so move we did.

I still remember very clearly our first day of school in Almyra, a town of 400. It was the month of May, close to the end of the school year, and perhaps that accounts for the bare feet and flip-flops, the sense of celebratory abandon. My mother dropped Bonzie and me off during recess, and what a recess it was! One girl was playing Tommy Roe's hit single "Dizzy" on a small record player; another girl, who had pink sponge rollers in her hair, was eating a lime lollipop that had turned her lips green; and the smell of homemade chicken and dumplings wafted out of the cafeteria. The only odd thing about the old school house was the fact that even though it sat in the middle of the Mississippi delta, there were no black students. But on that first day of school, everyone wanted to be our friend, and so Bonzie and I thought we had landed in a Delta paradise, especially after the misery of Parham.

That initial feeling of acceptance was short-lived, however. This was the beginning of what might be called a test of faith, the beginning of the loneliness and uncertainty that accompanies being out-of-place or "other" — a loneliness and uncertainty that has shadowed me throughout my life. With our white faces and Southern accents, we looked and sounded very much like the people around us, and yet we quickly came to be perceived as other because our family had rubbed elbows with Africans on one continent and African-Americans on another, because our family included a Native American child, and because our family had values, practices, and vocabulary that were different from the rest of the community. Bonzie and I were the weirdo kids who wrote plays about the Civil Rights Movement and acted them out with Barbie dolls, painting one doll black because it hadn't yet occurred to Mattel to produce one. We were the weirdo kids who, in the aftermath of the Kent State Massacre, created the Tree House Peace Club, which mostly entailed sitting in the tree house eating after-school snacks and singing Joan Baez songs. A couple of the neighborhood girls joined us, but I don't think they even knew where Vietnam was or that a war was waging there. Casting about for what to call us, then, the community came up with many names, the most polite of which was "Yankee," the favored term for anyone who is not southern. I was *in* the South but not *of* the South, and, in later years, I would be *in* the North but not *of* the North, destined to be without a "homeland."

The following year, as I was preparing to enter the sixth grade in Stuttgart, the School Board decided to make Holman Elementary, originally an all-black school on the other side of the tracks, the public school for all fifth and sixth graders, a decision that sent shock waves throughout the community and resulted in the sudden, panic-driven creation of a private school for whites who didn't want their children mingling with blacks. There was never any question that Bonzie and I would attend Holman, and it was there that I met a black student named Randall, who sat next to me through junior high and high school because our names both began with "Mc." Even as a sixth-grader, Randall carried a black briefcase and, when asked what it contained, answered with an air of mystery, "Confections." I liked Randall, his briefcase, and his wit.

But one day he turned to me and said, "Becky McLaughlin, did you know you marry the person you sit next to in school?"

"No," I said, shaking my head.

"It's a known fact," he replied. "Just check the statistics."

This gave me pause. I considered Randall a good friend, but I did not want to marry him. Did that make me a racist? I wondered. On another occasion when a black classmate asked to see my test paper during a moment in which the teacher's back was turned, I said, "No, that's cheating," but, again, I was led to ponder whether my refusal made me a racist. Living in a town guilty of no overt violence toward blacks, just a subtle undercurrent of separatism and something less than good will, these questions plagued me throughout my adolescent and teenaged years.

And then one day it happened. Instead of stewing in my own private musings about racism, I was forced to take a stand. If a sense of belonging had always eluded me, I was, as a senior in high school, given what felt like one final opportunity to be "in place." I was eating lunch with a friend who had made cheddar cheese and dill pickle sandwiches — her own invention, she told me. I liked the sharp taste of the cheese and the crunch of the pickle and felt pleased to be sharing her invention. She wore braces on her small, vulpine teeth, and I was fascinated by the way she managed to delicately tuck the sandwich between the wires and rubber bands in her mouth. As we talked about innocuous things like boys and our plans for college, I felt at ease. But then out of nowhere came a joke — a true non sequitur — and my friend was already laughing in delight as she began telling it. I realized immediately what kind of joke it was — a racist joke, one of the cruelest I've ever heard — and so I knew I had at most sixty seconds to figure out how to respond. Unfortunately, the joke was too simple and I was too smart to be able to pretend ignorance, and so I had only two real options. As the joke came to a close, my friend was choking with laughter, and I was paralyzed by indecision. She stopped laughing, narrowed her eyes, and looked at me suspiciously. "Don't you get it?" she asked, repeating the punch line, and so I laughed. For one split second I caught a glimpse of what it might feel like to belong, and then I just felt sick, as if I'd swallowed something that didn't agree with me — which, in fact, I had.

When I went north for college, I did not remain in touch with my friend. In fact, that lunch is my only real memory of her, but it's a useful memory because her joke and my response to it made clear that, for me, the price of belonging is too high and that, maybe, just maybe, being out of place is the place to be.

Works Cited

Miller, Perry. *Nature's Nation*. Cambridge: Harvard University Press, 1967.
Reed, Roy. *Faubus: The Life and Times of an American Prodigal*. Fayetteville: University of Arkansas Press, 1997.
Smith, Lillian. *Killers of the Dream*. New York: W. W. Norton, 1994.

Women's Work
and Working Women
by LESLIE HAYNSWORTH

My mother, born in Richmond, Virginia in 1941, was raised to believe what most white Southerners at that time believed to be true: that black people were inherently inferior to white people, and that keeping black people down at the bottom levels of society was thus the best thing for everybody. Then, in young adulthood, my mother encountered the Civil Rights Movement and came to believe that racial prejudice was wrong, and that its consequences, which were still so deeply embedded into the fabric of life in the South, were wrong too.

Redressing those wrongs, though, was complicated: when it was time for me to start school in 1972, in Columbia, South Carolina, desegregation had caused white flight to private schools to the extent that the public schools weren't very good. Like virtually everyone else who could afford to, my parents opted for the better educational outcomes that were promised by private schools. But my mother chose one of the two private schools in town that accepted black students too.

And she agonized over the issue of having a cleaning lady. Cleaning ladies were always black; they were called maids, and cleaning the homes of white women was just what black women did. My mother didn't want to be complicit in that lingering vestige of a social order she now felt was wrong. But when we moved to Columbia in 1971, she had three small children to keep up with and it really was difficult for her to manage everything on her own. With three children in tow, it was hard even to get basic errands done; if nothing else, she needed someone to be home with us for one day a week so she could go to the grocery store. So she hired Libby, who lived in rural Clarendon County, almost an hour away, and who got a ride to downtown Columbia every morning and then took the city bus to the home of whichever well-off white woman she was working for that day. Libby had two little boys of her own, about the same age as my brother and me, which would have made them five and three when she started working for us, and I don't know where they were or who was with them when she was with us. But I did realize, even as a child, that Libby had to get up really early in the morning to travel all that way to work each day, and that she then had a long ride home, after which she had household duties of her own. That didn't seem quite right. But it was just he way things were.

My father-in-law, who was born in Bennettsville, South Carolina in 1936, and who is one of the most fundamentally good-hearted people I know, says he can't understand why black women won't do this any more the way they used to, won't do for white women all the household work that few women really want to do. When he was young, he says, black women not only cleaned white households but also virtually raised white women's children. He sees my husband and me struggling to keep up with our lives, juggling our jobs and our two small boys and our household responsibilities, and he wishes for us that things could still be the way they used to be, because he knows that then our lives would be easier. He talks about this change in normative black female vocation not with anger but with what seems like genuine bafflement: the old system worked so well, and everyone seemed so happy with it at the time, so why would anyone want to change it? I've never heard him say anything overtly racist. But it's clear to me that for him certain accoutrements of racism appear both natural and desirable. It was racism that sustained the existence of a black underclass that had few options but to take on the kind of work no one really wanted to do, and to do it for wages low enough that even people like my parents, a homemaker and a college professor, could afford to hire both a cleaning lady and a yard man. It was racism, both institutional and informal, that foreclosed all the other opportunities that might have made a black woman like Libby say, no thank you, I don't think I want to ride 50 miles from my home each day so I can scrub some other lady's toilets and mind her children while she gets her hair done or plays tennis at the country club.

And because people like Libby weren't exactly in a position to complain about it, at least not to people like him, it's not hard to see how someone like my father-in-law could have felt that everyone, black and white, was happy with the whole situation. Even to someone like my mother, who grew up working-class, too poor to have a maid, and who initially felt so uncomfortable about the unfairness of hiring someone poorer than herself to do the work she'd been raised to believe was her responsibility, the white-family/black-maid dynamic must have come to seem normal, and maybe even okay, after a while. Everyone she knew had a maid. It may not have been right that women like Libby had to get up so early every morning and travel so far to clean other women's houses, but it was just the way things were. If my mother had refused to hire a maid, she could have felt that she was taking a principled stand against racial inequities, but her refusal wouldn't have done a thing to redress those inequities. It would only have made her own life harder. And what else was Libby going to do to support her family anyway?

Actually, at one point, when she was in her 40s, Libby did try to say no thank you to all that: she decided to become a nurse and enrolled in nursing classes at her local technical college. But even though by then, in the 1980s, it was perfectly possible for a black woman to become an RN, it wasn't possible for Libby. She'd been educated in the rural South in the 1940s and '50s, and she couldn't read or write well enough to manage the coursework. Within a year, she was back to cleaning houses. Today, she's in her mid–60s and she's still cleaning houses. If she ever in any way found the work rewarding, she must be tired of it by now.

And then compare Libby's vocational history with that of my friend Eileen. Eileen and Libby are about the same age, but Eileen is white. Like many women of my mother's generation, she got married when she was still in college. But the marriage didn't work out, and by the time she was 22, she was divorced and had two small children. While being the single mother of these two small children, Eileen went to graduate school at one of the South's most prestigious universities and earned a Ph.D. in English, then went on to have a long career as a college professor. That accomplishment is staggering to me. In all my years as a graduate student and then as an English professor, I've never met anyone else who even tried to earn a Ph.D. while being the primary caregiver for two preschoolers. Eileen says there was only one reason she was able to do it: her mother, who was comfortably off but by no means wealthy, was able to hire a black woman for next to nothing to care for Eileen's children while Eileen was in school.

So it was someone like Libby — someone whose own horizon of vocational possibilities had from her birth been squeezed down tight into the narrow range of maid/cook/babysitter — who made it possible for Eileen to accomplish so much. In Eileen's generation, women weren't supposed to become college professors. If they had pedagogical aspirations, they could be teachers for a few years before they had their kids. For someone like Eileen to become a college professor in the early 1970s, everything had to line up just right: she had to be very smart, she had to be tough, and she had to have help. She needed someone else to do for her all the things that otherwise would have consumed almost all the hours of her days: the cooking, the cleaning, the washing, the sewing; feeding the children and dressing them and bathing them and helping them go to the potty, and just plain paying attention to them when they want someone to talk to. She got that help from a black woman who had no choice but to work for the low wages Eileen's family could afford. And because she got that help and was therefore able to achieve so much, because she proved that, yes, in fact, a woman could be a college professor, it became considerably easier for women of my generation to imagine ourselves as college professors too. So when I entered graduate school in the early 1990s, I was, in a real sense, standing on the shoulders not just of women like Eileen herself but of the black women who freed women like Eileen from having to do all the endless round of quotidian tasks that would otherwise have kept them from climbing so high. Because this one group of women was trapped by their circumstances into having to take on hard and tedious work for low wages, women like me were able to get ahead in ways that many of us never otherwise could have.

It's different now. Because of people like my mother who pushed back against the prejudices with which they were raised, you can't just tell black women they have no choice but to be maids any more. At the women's college in Columbia, South Carolina where I taught from 2001–2007, almost half of the students are black now. In my mother's generation, none of them were. My former black students go on to be teachers and ministers and lawyers and businesswomen. None of them will ever be maids. But a lot of their grandmothers probably were.

So maids are in shorter supply now, and as a result have become more expensive. My husband is a doctor, and my father-in-law is right when he says that, if things were still the way they used to be, we could have easily afforded to have a black woman come in and "do" for us full time. Today, that would cost at least $500 a week, which would stretch our budget really tight. It's much cheaper to put our children in daycare and make do with having a cleaning lady come in one morning a week to scrub and mop for a few hours.

Cheaper, but not easier: if we had a maid who came every day, I'd never have to worry about how my work's going to get done when the children are sick and have to miss school. As it is, I'm constantly scrambling; for a number of years I taught at strange times so as to align my need for emergency babysitting as closely as possible to my mother-in-law's schedule. I've brought my mildly sick or recovering kids to class quite a number of times, which I felt okay about when I was at the women's college, because it seemed like a good object lesson for my students in the kinds of juggling acts they too were going to have to perform before long, but which is much less okay now that I'm a precariously positioned adjunct professor at a large university. And even though I do have a few hours a week of help with the housework, I still spend hours and hours of my time cleaning and washing and cooking. I never have as much time as I need to do all the work I'm supposed to do. After I had my second child, I was so overwhelmed that I had to cut back to working part time. And even so I was too stressed out, and so a year ago I left my tenure-track job and became a part-time instructor and a freelance writer. Things are less hectic now and I'm sleeping better at night, but I still feel like a professional failure: I gutted my way through one of the top Ph.D. programs in my field and then landed a real tenure-track teaching job; having come that far already, I should have been tough enough and resourceful enough to hold onto that job even with two small kids in tow.

And if I had a black woman to "do" for me every day, I could have. There would be no sink full of dishes waiting for me when I came home from work, no piles of laundry to be folded, probably not even any dinner to cook. I wouldn't have to disappear from work for three days at a time every time one of my children got an ear infection. Instead, I'd be able to live my professional life just like men do: I'd work during normal working hours, and then when I got home I'd be able to enjoy some relaxing time with my family.

So if things hadn't changed, if black women still had few other options, if I could hire a fulltime maid for a couple hundred dollars a week, would I? It's hard to say. Even though I, like my mother, would probably feel uncomfortable about it, it would still be so easy to justify: my maid would need the money and how else was she going to get it? And I might know that she, like Libby, was leaving her own children behind to care for my children every day, but if her presence in my home seemed like the best thing for my kids, that would be easy to justify too. How could I not act in the best interest of my children? Like my mother, I want to live in a world where everyone, male or female, black or white, has the same opportunities to achieve whatever they want to achieve in life. But getting ahead is still, in the end, a zero sum game: not everyone can be a college professor. Someone's still going to have to do the laundry and the dishes. And if I recognize that as a woman, I'm going to need some help to get where I want to go in life, it's hard to turn that help away. Even with the best of intentions, most of us are not going to act against our own self-interest, or the best interest of our families, so that someone else can get ahead.

Racial attitudes in the South may have changed a lot in the last 30 or 40 years, but as far as the material circumstances of our lives are concerned, we're still in a zero sum game. If you give women like Libby more options, if they can become nurses or teachers instead of cleaning ladies, then cleaning ladies are going to become scarcer, and to get one you'll have to pay her more, which in turn will mean that a whole stratum of people who used to be able to afford a cleaning lady won't be able to do so any more, and then their lives will become harder or at least less pleasant, insofar as they have to start doing a bunch of chores that they don't really want to do. Sometimes when I'm scrubbing pots at the kitchen sink, gritting my teeth and thinking about how much I hate cleaning the kitchen, I try to remind myself that the fact that I have to do it is in the abstract a good thing, that I've been pushed back into the kitchen so that my black students can be doctors and bankers and PR executives and foundation directors. I'm glad that my students have those opportunities. But the fact that they do makes my life a little harder.

And it's because it was in the end an accretion of what seemed like small difficulties — a dirty kitchen, a sick kid here and there, a pile of pajamas waiting to be folded — that forced me to scale back my own professional ambitions, I worry that even with all the ways that things have become more fair for African Americans, they're still not as fair as they seem. My black students do in theory have all the same options now that my white students do. But because more of them come from economically disadvantaged families, they're operating with less of a safety net. For them to succeed in big ways, everything has to line up just right: they have to be smart, they have to be tough, and they have to be lucky — lucky in the sense that nothing happens to derail their ambitions, that they don't get pregnant, or end up having to nurse a sick parent, or having to drop out of school to support their family when their father loses his job. Because unlike my friend Eileen, they're not going to have help, at least not the kind of help Eileen had. They're not going to be able to hire a black woman for a couple hundred dollars a week to come in and handle the family's needs for them so that they can finish school and get ahead.

Last year, I had an African-American student who was the single mother of a 1-year-old son. She was in college full time, and at the end of her school day, she went to work full time to pay for her son's daycare and all of his and her own other expenses. One day, she had to bring her son to class, and it was obvious that he was a happy, well-adjusted kid. He was also a lot better behaved than my three-year-old had been when I brought him to the same class a week earlier. So my student is doing great as a mom, doing everything she can for her child, and doing everything she can to stay in school so that he and she can both have a better future. But she was, patently, always exhausted. And her work in my class wasn't as good as it could have been. She was very smart and a naturally gifted writer. But when did she have time to polish her essays, to make them as good as they could be? She's smart enough that I have no doubt she'll be able to graduate even if she can't put as much effort into her classes as she should. But she won't graduate with the grades she's capable of earning, and that will mean she won't have all the options she was innately capable of having. Just think how different things would have been for her if she, like Eileen, had been able to find a maid to look after her son for next to nothing.

And even for the lucky ones, the black students for whom everything does line up just right, there are still all the lingering vestiges of racism to be dealt with. A few years ago at the women's college where I used to teach, the leadership of the Black Student Association published a six-page list of concerns that included issues like these: "African American students have seen and experienced professors 'calling out' or belittling African American students that have asked questions about the material that is being taught; some African American students commented that every time they walk down the halls in their dorm, white students slam their doors when they see the African American students approaching their rooms; many times white students and black students will not speak to each other."

As an obstacle to getting an education or achieving professional success, being belittled by a professor for asking a question may not be the same as having to raise children, attend school and hold down a job all at the same time. But the experiences described in the students' list of concerns do, on a deep, existential level, create discomfort and induce stress. And when a college student is stressed out about one thing, it's that much harder to focus on the other things she's trying to accomplish, and when she and every other student of similar ability are all struggling for the same prizes that only some of them will be able to get, the same limited number of places in medical school or graduate school, say, even small bumps in the road can have disproportionately large consequences: because the white girl down the hall hasn't had to worry about what the color of her skin signifies to her professors, she's had more mental energy to apply to her class work, and as a result, her grades are just that much better; and because she's felt more at home on campus, she's amassed an impressive list of extracurricular activities, joining clubs where her black hallmate was never sure she was welcome. So there's a kind of continual low-grade friction against that, at least in the aggregate, rubs harder against young black women than against young white women, and so in the aggregate it's still going to be easier for white girls to achieve their full potential, to get the competitive edge that puts them on the fast track to the brightest future they're capable of having. And it's not like my black students will have to become maids like their grandmothers did, but all the same, when I see what they're still up against, I can't help knowing that most of them will never get quite as far in life as they could if their race truly didn't matter any more.

When 45 percent of the students at a private women's liberal arts college in South Carolina are African American, I can't help but think that we've come a long way since Libby was a young woman. But when I listen to my students talk about their lives, I can't help seeing that things still aren't as equal as they seem on the surface. Even when my white students are more enlightened than their parents were (and sometimes they're not), you can't expect them to let go of their own opportunities, or in any other way deliberately make their own lives harder, just so someone else with a different skin color can get ahead. Even my mother, who didn't think it was right that black women had to work as white women's maids, still hired a maid when her life became too difficult without one.

My mother wanted to take a stand for justice. She wanted to not commit this act of hiring a maid that she saw as perpetuating a retrogressive social order. But in the end she did hire a maid, and in her mind that made her complicit with much that she felt was wrong.

What my mother did accomplish, though, may, in light of where we are now, be far more significant. The tempting thing, once you've done something you feel to be wrong, is to rationalize it, to find a way to justify it, so that you can tell yourself it's okay after all. In the 1970s, when almost everything in our world still reflected a Jim Crow division of labor and resources, and when almost everyone we knew saw that as being just the way things were, that justification could have come easily for my mother. Instead, my mother held on to her discomfort and vocalized her feelings of complicity. In so doing, she passed on to me a keener awareness that what looks normal and natural on the surface — that virtually every white family in our neighborhood had a maid — may still not be right. She cracked the smooth surface of my world where having a black maid was just what you were supposed to do and taught me that what lay beneath that surface was more complicated and more fraught than it seemed. It would be easy now, when young black Southerners do in theory have the same options and opportunities that young white Southerners do, to see our world as having finally become fair and equal. It's thanks to my mother that I can see that we still have a way to go.

1975 Wasn't a Very Good Year

by GEORGENE BESS MONTGOMERY

My memories of my childhood are divided into two periods — before and after my father's death, one a time of careless and carefree youth and the other a time of unmitigated terror, menaced by the KKK and racist neighbors. I grew up on a farm in rural South Georgia, in a small town (a misnomer perhaps) called Glenwood, which has one traffic light, a small grocery store, two gas stations, and a hospital that serves the whole of Wheeler County. I grew up about ten miles from the city limits on a dirt road, a road so narrow that two cars can't pass each other; one has to pull over to let the other go by. When it rains, the red Georgia clay makes for some hazardous driving conditions for folk who don't know how to drive in it. Despite its hazard on the road, the rain smells so sweet, and when mingled with the dirt, the scent is practically divine. When the road is dry, the sand, found at the other end of the road, can be equally hazardous, too, as it once was for me when I was driving too fast and lost control of my compact car.

Barefoot and carefree, my siblings and I scampered up and down that dirt road that went past our house. During the summers, we lived off the fruit of the land, much preferring it to the hand-grown, hand-picked vegetables from the garden. Each day brought a sense of adventure. We were never afraid of any potential danger, although we were always cautioned to be on guard by Mommy and our older siblings. We thought nothing of walking through the woods in a constant search for adventure and goodies. We didn't worry about snakes, wild hogs, or strangers. In fact, snakes, I think, were probably afraid of us. When snakes saw us coming, they would glide quickly in the other direction, but we always managed to hem them up, taunting them with sticks and stones. Once we gave away one such snake to a man who was out gathering snakes for the Rattlesnake Round-Up. Perhaps we inherited this lack of fear and intense dislike of snakes from our mother who, having lost a son to a rattlesnake bite, would viciously beat any snake she saw.

Our mouths watering, we feasted daily on sweet grass, gooseberries, huckleberries, plums, peaches, scuppernongs, muscadines, blackberries, watermelons, tomatoes, cucumbers, and freshly dug sweet potatoes. We drank delicious blackberry jam — whole blackberries and the juice of squashed blackberries, mixed with sugar. We also ate dirt, not the dirt of our mudpies, but the dirt travelled in on the harrow when Daddy turned the soil over to ready it for planting. It had a cool, sweet, metallic taste. Daddy would chuckle to see us eating the dirt, saying "That's what wrong with city children, they don't eat dirt!" I probably ate enough for them too.

We were seldom bored for there was always some mischief to get into, like the time we decided to wash the chimney and impress Mommy with our industriousness. What we didn't realize was the greasy nature of soot. Soon tired of washing and washing with no tangible results, we abandoned that project. Black from head to foot with soot, we got into the bathtub. However, instead of washing off our bodies and running into the drain with the dirty water, the soot stuck to the walls, the tub, and the floor. Horrified at the trouble we were sure to be in and the whipping we were sure to get, we frantically wiped down the walls and the floor, and the tub but to no avail. And just as we fearfully anticipated, we got a whipping that night!

Or like the time we decided to run away because our older sister Lynise wouldn't let us in the house as she angrily admonished, "You either stay in or stay OUT!" Out we chose to stay until we wanted to go back in. So, we put our heads together and a few parts from various items and toys to make us a car to drive away in. We would fix her, we reasoned. We found a 4×4 plank. We nailed the seat from our youngest brother GB's toy tractor to the board and a tin lid from the syrup can to make a steering wheel. For the finishing touch, we took the wheels from our youngest sister Ava's baby carriage. Excited and ready to go, we carried the "car" to the road, got on, and prepared to go. With the weight of five young bodies and a plank, the fragile carriage wheels collapsed. Disappointed, we sulked to the front porch, fussing about our mean sister, "witch" we called her. We even rode the hogs. We would tie an ear of corn to a string which was then tied to the end of a stick like a fishing pole. We then called the hogs — "Here Pig! Here Pig!" Enticed by the corn, the hogs would come to nibble. Once the hog was nibbling, one of us would jump on his back for a ride. The ride seldom lasted long, shorter than a bullrider on an untamed bull.

We were thrown in a deep puddle of hog mud, hog wallow we called it. Stinking and a mess, we would get up and try it again!

Having only ourselves and the occasional visitor or cousin visiting from "Up North" to play with, we invented our own games, adding to the roster of such games as hide-and-go seek, tag, dodgeball, and our favorite, "Red Rover, Red Rover, send Georgene right over!" After the rain, we would swim naked in the ditches dug deeper by the bulldozer the previous day in anticipation of the rain or the bridge (not really a bridge — just a slight creek that ran under the road and existed on both sides of the road). When we were completely bored, we would put our heads to ground, the way heard we Native Americans did to hear who was coming, and listen for trucks passing by on Highway 19, the major road, at the end our dirt road.

But life on the farm was not all play. We had to work too. And work we did. We had to feed the hogs, pick and shell peas and butterbeans, row after never-ending row, backbreaking labor. We picked so many we would be picking them in our sleep. We dreamed about shelling peas and beans! Then there was the okra that made us itch. We had to pick corn and shuck it, sometimes eating it raw; it was so sweet and milky. Then there was the tobacco, a summer-long project. First, we had to plant it. Then weed it, with our hands no less. Then sucker it, that is remove from the stalk "suckers" that imitated the tobacco leaves but absorbed all of the nutrients from it. Finally, it was time to crop the tobacco, taking the leaves from the stalk and putting them on a tobacco stick by wrapping about three leaves at time with tobacco twine and tying them to the stick. Then the tobacco sticks were hung in the barn where the tobacco was cooked. Ahh, the smell of cooked tobacco — MMMM Good! After the tobacco was cooked, it was time to take it off the stick and place it on the tobacco sheet to be taken to the market. Like with the peas, beans, corn, we saw the tobacco in our sleep too.

Work was always mixed with fun though. The hands hired to help us were cousins, classmates, adults, and friends of our parents. There were also plenty of stories, fights, arguments, gossip that kept us thoroughly entertained! One day while we were cropping tobacco, our neighbor Mrs. Bee was so busy talking that she was not taking the tobacco that my sister Lydia was cropping. Her lap getting fuller and fuller while Mrs. Bee was busy talking, Lydia jumped up from her seat, spilling the tobacco on the ground, and stomped home. Everyone was stunned into silence, including Mrs. Bee. Earl Troup, our first cousin, stopped the tractor. Daddy got in his truck, went to the house, and brought Lydia back. There was not a whole lot of talking after that, at least not that day!

Although I loved summertime, I loved school too. I was so excited about going to kindergarten. I got to attend school with my big sisters and brother — Wheeler County Training School! My first teacher, Miss Howard, was so sweet and kind. I never forgot her and was thrilled when she later married my cousin. Because I had a speech impediment — I could only pronounce the letter N; for example, "Nonny, Ni nant nome noonies nand nilk" (translated: Mommy, I want some cookies and milk) — I went to speech therapy where Mrs. Thurman taught me the proper way to pronounce vowels and consonants and to enunciate my words. The puzzled looks on people's faces as they tried to figure out what I was saying soon turned to being impressed as I became the most articulate little girl they knew. In first grade I wanted to be the President's wife! When I started third grade, the schools integrated. Wheeler County Training School became simply Wheeler County Elementary, Middle, Junior, and High School. In 1972, the year I entered fourth grade, Shirley Chisholm became the first African-American woman to run for President of the United States. During the mock class elections, I, of course, voted for Shirley Chisholm. When my teacher noted that I voted for her because she was Black, I responded, "and that's why you didn't vote for her!" I was, after all, Sarah Bess' child!

Yep, life was pretty good. Then came 1975, the year my father died, the year everything changed. I was twelve years old. It was then I learned about racism, fear, and terror. Sure, I knew about racism from Mommy and Daddy's stories. Years earlier, because there was no school bus for Black children, Daddy had bought a school bus to drive them school, charging them a dime a week for gas. Once, Mommy, pregnant with my sister Lynise, her baby Sheila in her arms, and her oldest son Larry holding her hand, beat up a White man for forcing a little Black girl off the sidewalk. She handed Sheila to her sister-in-law and grabbed the man by his collar and commenced to beating him with her fist. Later, she and her cousin waited at the gate for the Klan to ride. They didn't. Apparently they knew not to mess with Sarah!

I already knew about racism from the segregated movie theater where we went to see, ironically, *Song of the South*, and from our school dances. We had to go to the back of the dark theater, sit on hard, wooden seats. We could only buy popcorn and soda. However, in the front of the theater, the Whites Only entrance, on display were candy bars, popcorn, a variety of candy, chips, and sodas. We felt the utter injustice of it and vowed to never attend that theater again. And we didn't. For our school dances, the principal declared, "No mixed couples on the dance floor." Hurt and angry, we responded with a feeble attempt at humor, "We don't want to dance with Whites anyway; they can't even dance." Our white neighbors, the Artwrights*, my older siblings' classmates, would ride by on a truck with a shot gun, yelling, "Niggers." Despite the landmark 1954 *Brown vs. Board of Education* decision to end school segregation, we attended a segregated school — Wheeler County Training School — until 1970, when I was in the second grade. Sure, I knew fear because I was afraid of whippings, not that it kept me from getting into trouble. What I didn't know was pure, unmitigated hate, fear so tangible I could taste it, and terror that plagued my waking moments and my sleep.

My father, George, had bought our farm years before I was born. A White man was selling the land, but no one would meet his asking price. Plotting that the thought of a "Colored" man buying his property would inspire the Whites to meet his price, he asked Daddy to offer to buy. What he did not expect was that my Daddy was serious about his offer. He tried his best to get Daddy to change his mind. At the urging of Mommy, Daddy bought the land, much to the dismay and chagrin of many Whites who were mortified that a Colored man, a nigger, would own property. Significantly, it wasn't until after Daddy died that they most clearly revealed themselves but were not dressed in white sheets. Their agenda? Run that nigger woman and her children off the land.

And so their reign of terror began. First, it was showing up at the house when no one was there but us children — there were five of us at the time, four girls, ages 15, 14, 12, 10, and one boy, age 9 — to intimidate us. Then at night, a truckload of White men would pull up and just sit in the yard smoking cigarettes while we slept; well, actually, their presence murdered our sleep. The next morning there were piles of cigarette butts on the ground in the yard as if it were a giant ashtray. Throughout the night, people would ride slowly by our house with the car lights off. Hearing the car but seeing no lights, we were terrified. With hearts pounding and eyes widened, we whispered to each other, as if the driver could hear us, "Do you hear that?" Our hogs and cows were poisoned. Lying beside the poisoned hogs and cows were dead buzzards. The Georgia Bureau of Investigations (GBI) investigated, but nothing came of it. One time our cows got out. A racist neighbor loaded them onto his truck and set them loose at the river. Mommy pressed charges against him, and he had to pay her for the lost cows. Our stock bull was poisoned with potash. Then our

---

*With the exception of siblings and cousins, the names have been changed to protect both the innocent and the not so innocent.

woods would mysteriously catch on fire and burn. I remember vividly the night our White neighbor came to tell us our field was on fire. He said he could not in good conscience let it burn and not notify us. He put out the fire before the crops were destroyed; only the fence was damaged. Another time our field was set afire. Fortunately, a friend of the family was passing by, saw the flames, and put it out by digging a row between the burning crops so that the fire would not spread to the rest of the field. News of the fire further exacerbated our fears. That night we expected a cross to burn in our yard. It didn't. A burning field instead of a burning cross was much more devastatingly effective.

My older brother, Larry, having graduated from college, came home to farm. He would be out late at night plowing on the tractor. My siblings and I couldn't sleep for worrying about his safety. Unable to sleep and finding no comfort in mashing my pillow that I had since a baby or in sucking my tongue, the companion act, I would have horrific visions of my brother lynched, tarred-and-feathered, hanging from some tree, and that we might (or might not) find him days later, his body so badly mutilated he would be unidentifiable.

Coming home from school was no better. Although the nightmares of the night were gone, they were replaced with daymares; for then, too, we agonized over the realistic possibility that we would pass the fields and see my brother dead, bloody and bruised from beatings or find him and Mommy lying dead in the yard from shotgun blasts or swinging from the many trees in our yard. We were also afraid each time the bus rounded the curve near our house. Each day we expected the house to be in flames. We released bated breaths only when the bus stopped in front of the house, and we saw it still standing, smoke-free. Our fears were not ungrounded, for we saw Larry constantly harassed and jailed by the police for no reason. Whenever he drove to town, the police would follow him, waiting, perhaps hoping and praying he would make some mistake, not use his turn signal or drive a mile over the speed limit. When he didn't do anything wrong, they still stopped and arrested him.

The FmHA (Farmers Home Administration) participated in this racist treatment also by denying Mommy and other Black farmers loans while granting them to Whites. In 2009, Mommy was awarded a settlement in the Black Farmers' civil suit against the FmHA. However, that award comes too little, too late. Because of the denial, we had to take out a much larger loan, to save the farm from foreclosure. The settlement did not cover the cost of the new loan, so we are still struggling to pay off the loan, money we would not have had to borrow had FmHA done right the first time.

Because we were relatively isolated — in a small town and then way out in the country — we didn't hear much news of the outside world. We could only get two channels on our television, one of which was PBS — we watched *Sesame Street*, *Electric Company*, and *Zoom* way past the recommended age! We could get the Lawrence Welk show — "Good Night, Until We Meet Again. Adios, Au Revoir, Auf Wiedersehn!" — but not much else. As children, we weren't interest in the news, but even if we were, that was the channel that didn't come through clearly, even with the rabbit-eared antennae. Consequently, we didn't hear much about the Civil Rights Movement, except from our older siblings, but we were engaged in our own Civil Rights Movement, at school, on the bus, at the hands of racist teachers, a racist bus driver, and racist bus riders.

Practically every day I had to beat up a White boy for calling me a nigger. When the driver turned a blind ear to the name calling, I took matters into my own hands. Our school bus driver, Mr. Manford, seemed to just hate us, "them uppity niggers." "Them independent Besses" he derisively called us. While driving the bus, he would just stare at us in the mirror, his eyes hate-filled, skin beet red. We would stare back at him defiantly. When we got on the bus but before we were seated, Manford would lurch forward trying to make us fall. As we scrambled to regain our balance and find a seat, he would smile smugly. Manford continued his ill-treatment of us in the afternoon. As soon as we exited the bus, he would take off, burning rubber on a dirt road, leaving us covered in dust. Expressing our fear, anger, and pent-up frustrations, my youngest brother George (GB) would rap Grandmaster Flash's "The Message": "Don't push me/ I'm close to the edge, trying hard not to lose my head. It makes me wonder sometimes how I keep from going under." However, we were Besses; despite the wish that we would, we were not going anywhere and certainly not under.

The Argons, a white family who rode our bus, would all sit together five in one seat so as not to have to share a seat with "a nigger," they said. Recognizing this, we — Lydia, Millicent, Ava, GB, and I — would each take a seat. Thus five seats, in addition to the ones occupied by the other Black passengers, were no longer available, and they chose to either stand or sit all bunched up. One day while getting off the bus, Charles Argon knocked my book out of my lap and called me a nigger as he got off the bus. Angry that he dared to call me a nigger and knocked my book to the floor, a double insult, I jumped up, got off the bus, too, and slapped the living daylights out of him. My hand left a red print on his face for days. The next morning, his family was waiting in the yard for the school bus with a long, iron pole, intending to harm us. That didn't happen, although we were ready to take them on. Embracing and celebrating our Blackness and seeking to counter the constant racial notion of White beauty and purity and Black ugliness and powerlessness, we defiantly rewrote the oft repeated saying, "If you white, you alright. If you brown, stick around. If you yellow, you mellow. If you black, step back." Instead, we chanted, "Black is beautiful, Brown is it. Yellow is mellow. White ain't S —-!"

We eventually got our own school bus, a bus for just five Black children. Finally sick and tired of the Lenny Manford's racist treatment of us, Mommy went to the school superintendent and threatened not to vote for him if he didn't get her children off that bus. Shortly thereafter we had a new bus driver and a new bus. On that narrow dirt road the two buses would meet each other and one would have to pull over for the other.

I also watched the White school teachers ignore the raised hands of Black students and instead call upon the White students for the answers. Wanting to "track" me in the slower learning class, my teacher ignored my high test score and attempted to place me at the table with the slower learning students. I simply ignored his request and refused to move. Perhaps aware of the error of his ways, he didn't fight but allowed me to stay where I was.

Growing up in the South, a place both so beautiful and yet so ugly, informed my notions about race, racism, and White people. Not all of my experiences with Whites were unpleasant. When news of Mr. Manford's mistreatment of us spread, many of the Whites in the community banned together and stopped patronizing his store. In contrast to Mr. Manford, the racist bus driver, whose daughter was my classmate and friend, there was Mr. Arpton, the husband of my third grade teacher who was kind and loving to ALL of her students. When the Argons met us at the bus with the iron pole, it was Mr. Arpton who would not allow them on the bus. There was Mrs. Oke, the wife of the principal and an English teacher herself, who submitted my poetry to a literary journal and gifted me a subscription. It was our White neighbor, Mr. Eeks, father of our classmates, who informed us that night that our field was on fire. My White classmates, were, by and large, open and friendly.

However, those acts of kindness and friendships did little to offset the terror of my youth or change my overall negative opinion about Whites. That sentiment assuaged somewhat when I attended Georgia Southern College in 1981, and shared a dorm and classes with Whites, whom I realized were not all monsters. Yet, even that experience does not mitigate the discomfort I sometimes feel when I walk into a drinking establishment peopled by Whites. My concern that I would be called a nigger by a drunken White often keeps me from entering. When my daughter was a child and would naturally seek the companionship of White children while we were out shopping, I would always cringe, expecting her to be rejected by the White parents. Wanting to protect her from that rejection, I would often simply redirect her attention.

It is indeed amazing how time does change things. I saw one of the Argons a few years ago. She was so friendly. She gave me a hug. I thought to ask her where is all of the hate but decided against it. I guess it was gone along with time. About five years ago, I also saw Mr. Manford at his country store (which is no longer open). Perhaps feeling guilty and ashamed of his atrocious behavior and reformed by time, he was gracious and asked how everyone was doing and even stated it was good to see me. I asked about his daughter, and he gladly shared with me news about her. And one of the Artwrights is leasing our land to farm.

Despite the racism and the daily and nightly terrors, we survived. We all drew strength from our memories of Daddy, his Spirit, and Mommy's fortitude, courage, and refusal to back down or back up. Through example and their stories, Mommy taught us to stand up and stand tall, never to give in or give up. We were intimately connected to the land through our blood, sweat, tears, the memories of the good times, the fun, the fruit, and the dirt and that connection was deep, unyielding, and unbreakable. These experiences drew us closer together as a family.

Now when we go home today, we can fully enjoy the feel of the green grass under our bare feet, inhale the sweet, sweet smell of the fresh country air, take our children down the dirt roads and through the fields, telling them stories of our childhood without the fear and terror of old. The White villains of my youth all seem to have either reformed, moved on or moved away. I am left with memories of my two childhoods, one full of laughter, mischief, and fun, and the other of fear, racism, and terror. However, the childhood I carry most with me and share with my daughter Zora Indigo is the one filled with sweet memories — the sweet smell of the rain, the sweet taste of wild fruit, and the sweet sounds of laughter. Many of the wild fruits that served as our feasts are no longer there, destroyed in the name of progress and neglect. But still there are the plums, blackberries, peaches, and scuppernongs, sweet grass, and dirt. I haven't eaten any dirt in a long time. Maybe I will have a bite with my daughter so she can grow up right. She is, after all, a city girl.

The Absence of Water

by Glenis Redmond

Growing up my family never vacationed and, though the word existed in the Redmond family lexicon, we only spoke the word "vacation" by rote as if it had no real significance or real meaning in our lives. Only the school calendar held the promise of release during the months of November and December, as well as the summertime vacation months. Our elementary hearts counted on vacating our Monday through Friday routines, as well as our minds. We would do what children did best. We would play endless games of Spades, Monopoly, Prison Ball and our favorite card game that ended with the challenge, *I declare war!* As a band of warriors we did declare war with our last day of school palpable chant, "No more teachers, no more books, no more teachers dirty looks." We knew we would celebrate the coming Holidays with our whole selves and plan on spending as many hours with our friends, and beg our parents as much as possible to do sleepovers. On the day that marked the beginning of vacation my heart would almost beat out of my chest, whether that was due to school letting out or the sugary snacks I consumed in class at the holiday party, I could not tell you, all I know is that we could barely contain our glee in the halls. We felt liberated and freed.

Yet, for us, the Redmonds, the bus ride was just that, a ride home. Home to that place we did not vacate for new territories or for respite or luxury's sake. We never wore a badge, sewn with pity about this fact. It was a given, a non-issue for it was the way of our lives, never questioned or examined.

Many of my classmates did vacation, if only on day trips. I would hear them discussing their forays and talk about their swimming and boating expeditions. Lake Hartwell was a location talked about frequently. It was a chief vacation spot for many of my white classmates. It was only thirty minutes away from where we lived but in our minds it could have

109

been a continent away. Our attitudes and retorts to questions about our vacation when we returned to school were resolved like the sentiments in Reuben Jackson's poem, "Sunday Brunch."

> And where
> do your parents
> summer?
> she asked
> him.
>
> the front porch,
> he replied.

We were indeed front porch people, but not fully limited to our stoops. My family trekked many miles. We experienced many cultures, encountered other customs and touched down on several foreign lands. These stints were due to my father being enlisted in the Air Force. Yet, in Spain, Morocco, France, Italy and many destinations across the United States, we never went camping, visited resorts or portaged into the country. This sort of outing was not in my families' repertoire. My sharecropper-born parents preferred to stick close to their routines, which were solidly linked to home and base. If it weren't for my adventurous 4th and 5th grade teachers, Ms. Anderson and Ms. Vann, I would have never witnessed the David in Florence, the Sistine Chapel in Venice, the ruins of Pompeii and the city lights of Rome. My parents, though they left the South, carried the boundaries of Jim Crow. It was alive within them for good reasons. It would take me years to understand their reticent and hesitant attitudes. Personal growth and maturity would later afford me the ability to gain a healthier perspective on the impact of poverty and racism on my family as a whole. Yet, my siblings and I did as children do, we challenged and prodded our parents.

Many years later I married interracially, which caused somewhat of a stir but not too much of one, because all of my siblings had dated across racial lines, so they had already broken racial barriers in our household. I married into a family that vacationed annually on South Carolina shores, I felt like both an interloper and an intruder, not only because of race but because of cultural differences as well. At the beach my internal alarm system threatened and I thought I would be spotted as a fraud or worse hand-cuffed and imprisoned for committing the most terrible crime, according to my mother: doing nothing. As I tried to ease my weary mind and slather my mahogany body down with SPF 40 on the tawny sands, while assuming the horizontal position in the shade under an umbrella rented for my use mostly, I could hear Jeanette Redmond, my mother, in my head like on every Saturday morning, "You don't have nothing to do? I'll find you something to do." There at this particular edge of the world, I met my own personal precipice and I knew it would be a life-long lesson, how to relax and go with the flow. The old cliché, you can lead a horse to water but you can't make him drink, defined me sufficiently. I was a stubborn and well-taught workhorse. Dipping my toe in the water for relaxation's sake was so foreign from the driven path of my life. Relaxation and taking care of my psyche seemed distant from the work ethic my mother poured into me. From the beginning I was an internally driven child. I remember cleaning my mother's house from top to bottom regularly, without being asked at the age of twelve, and when she began working at the Model Coat Factory, I would have supper ready after she worked twelve-hour long shifts. I had already learned I had to earn my keep and establish my worth in this world, a subtle or not so subtle message I had already absorbed.

I had the good girl mantra running through my veins, which flowed with the hope of never causing my parents a moment's worry. I began babysitting at eleven. Then, for my first real job, I donned a drab brown polyester pantsuit and worked for ARA Food Services at my father's job, the Michelin Tire Corp. There I flipped burgers and grilled hotdogs for the workers on their lunch break. Eventually, I progressed to an orange polyester smock at the Family Mart grocery store where I worked as a cashier. I never wanted to ask them for necessities they could not afford like brake shoes for the Plymouth Duster or ask them to pay to repair the driver's side door that swung open every time I took a left hand turn. Of course, I took my life in my own hands every time I drove, but this was the way of the world or so I thought. I had internalized some of the impact of poverty but not to a whole degree. I had enough will and faith not to cower to the full range of learned helplessness. I had an inner resource that was not of my own making.

"Stacked"

The cotton I carry is stacked
stacked on my mama's back.
The invisible load I tote, topped
by her mama's and her mama's mama
threatens to sickle my spine.

So, I weave their stories of the rented land
into it, with this strand I become a whole bowl
cradling strength. These lines define my backbone,
it lengthens even with red clay weight of it.
Mama told me her fingers were never nimble enough
To keep up only gathering 250 pounds of cotton a day.
She says, *your grandma picked 400, her mama 500.*
They were big women,
even with knees wrapped in rags
crawling down rows,
they towered.

Maybe my parents would have helped, but I knew they were strained financially so I did not want to add to their burden by asking for luxuries. I went to work so I too could sport a cap and gown on graduation day, and I could wear a class ring like many of my classmates. What my parents could not afford, I did not fret over; I went to work and bought what I needed. I went from high school to college to graduate school to wife to mother without much breathing in between. It seemed I was going with the flow, yet I never stopped to ask what was good for my soul. I was definitely on dry land spirit-wise with doing.

Like many, I did not escape my childhood unscathed. At age twenty-eight I was diagnosed with Fibromyalgia, a chronic-syndrome musco-skeletal illness that attacks both the muscles and the immune system resulting in constant pain and flu-like symptoms.

Louise Hay, author of *You Can Heal Your Life*, wrote, "It is an illness fraught with emotional turmoil that cause muscles to knot in pain. A person is under this type of duress usually experiences muscle tension, stiffness and mostly pain. It is felt in the fibrous tissues, usually deep within the muscles, yet there is nothing wrong with the muscles themselves." Stiffness is often a result of rigid, stiff thinking. Tension, fear, and holding on result in the body cramping and gripping." I happened to believe where I came from did not cause, yet did add to this chronic condition.

Piedmont, South Carolina, was and is a racially inflamed region like much of the South. I did not endure what my parents endured but the lines of Jim Crow still apply to that region. Crosses burned in my parent's neighborhood even up to a few years ago; the Confederate flag still waves upon the state capital grounds. Greenville County was the last in the country to honor the holiday for Martin Luther King, Jr. This year where my brother worked not too far from our family home, someone took effort to scrawl in graffiti-style on the buildings and van: "Niggers, Jews and Cubans go home."

I was a highly sensitive child and growing up in this heat I felt I had internalized shame, hate and guilt. I was ill equipped to face the daily hate that still exists. Poverty and racism went hand in hand and it took me years to give voice to this psychological oppression. I had a hard time understanding the contradictory messages in the Bible Belt. "Love Thy Neighbor ... only if they look like you" seemed to me an incongruent message. When my parents relocated to their hometown of Greenville from Europe they had a hard time explaining the segregation and the hate still prevalent in the '70s to my twelve-year-old self. I tried to convey the vapid sentiment in a poem.

"Benediction"

We took back roads cutting cross-country
traveling from one small road to another
snaking from Moonville to Mauldin.
My big brother Willie and I rode
while the blue Duster began stuttering a dubious rattle,
sputtering to a stop.
It ended on a small rural track of road called Conastee,
a quarter mile stretch riddled with seven steeples,
each pointing a path to God:
First Baptist, Church of God, Deliverance of God,
United Methodist, Reedy River Presbyterian,
Conastee Fellowship Hall and McBee United Methodist.
Surely we were cloaked by the protection of the Lord,
as we knocked on the first door we saw,
a sweet grandma looking lady
opening her door like a smile
granting us a Samaritan's Act
by letting us use her phone.
Her words spilling over us like Gospel, even today.
Hurry night's about to fall.
You two are not safe around here.

Maybe there is no direct correlation from growing up in an unhealthy South with vicious attitudes to my chronic illness, yet I metaphorically and spiritually, I have been impacted and I have ingested the toxicity of this hatred. Racism and hate act as devices to constrict. It is telling that Fibromyalgia as a condition consist of a clenching and a involuntary tightness of muscle, it feels like a holding on, on the verge waiting for the next negative action or event to happen. My main way to escape was not to conform to the rigid and cramped space, but to learn to flow and live life fluidly and effortlessly. I did this through reading and writing. Poetry became my outlet at an early age. From the article titled, "Fibromyalgia: Enigma and the Stigma," Dr. Stephen Stahl reports, "Fibromyalgia is considered by some to be the result of unconscious conflicts manifesting themselves as physical symptoms, with pain serving as a somatic metaphor for unhappiness and a life that is not working out." I found it ironic when I sought medical help one of the chief remedies my doctors prescribed was water. Drink plenty of it. Soak in it and float in it. They purported heated water would relax and soothe the muscles. In this remedy lay one major problem. I could not swim. So baths, hot tubs and jacuzzis became my water bodies of choice.

The Redmond family did not do vacations nor did we do water. My parents did not swim, dip or dive in lakes, oceans, rivers or pools; therefore their children were not schooled to either. My parents were raised in the Jim Crow landlocked Greenville and Waterloo, South Carolina, and they had their own turbulent views of water. They had no access to pools or swimming holes (this meant private land) and they never thought of water as a recreational source. Water was for drinking, bathing, fishing or cooking. My parents' discussion around water went much like this. "Stay away from water, you will drown." Right underneath that admonition there were stories and within these stories the underlying theme was fear. In regards to water my parents would say, " You know what they do to us with water and trees." Then from some mystical scary place, pictures would emerge of Emmett Till and black men hanging from trees. So when I heard Billie Holiday's "Strange Fruit" for the first time. I knew the eerie song was not a far off reality. The very ground and the water spoke of this. This message was planted within my siblings and myself purposely. Though I knew my parents were trying to build our defense mechanism with their warnings, this fear found its way into my bones extending like an unforgettable liquid into my nighttime dreams. I carried it everywhere I went.

Sometime in the Seventies my parents became more modern and lax. Away from the South where the bases were fully integrated they started experimenting with stepping out of their comfort zones. They went against the grain of their upbringing and allowed us to go to the swimming pool on Aviano Air Force Base with our friends. They never asked if we could swim or sought out swimming lessons for us. This too was the way of our world, no instruction manuals or guidance. You just jump in and either float or sink. I remember on a dare I jumped in the pool, determined to touch the bottom of the deep end. It took me so long to pierce the surface, the blond-haired teenage lifeguard was readying to jump in and perform some life-saving technique on me. He was so frustrated and alarmed he blurted, "You are banned from the deep end forever." He had no clue that I did need this warning because my lungs had already gotten that point across as they filled to their capacity. My body aching from exhaustion and from the life review I had witnessed on my ascent had already taught me a valuable swimming lesson, a life lesson: water and I did not mix, further adding validity to my parent's admonition. This incident also gave credence to the racist 1969 study titled "The Negro and Learning to Swim: The Buoyancy Problem Related to Reported Biological Difference," which surmised that blacks can't swim. From then on I took this erroneous scientific claim to heart.

So there is no wonder why on the South Carolina shores I could not abandon my twenty-three-year water theology. I sat oceanside not even entertaining the idea of getting in and when I did my fear of being swept away kept me from enjoying the water. Each wave that hit I knew a jellyfish or shark lurked in the murky waters. I sat on the shores and struggled even still, do what most vacationers do by doing nothing.

Especially after becoming a young mother of twins even my vacation was always packed full of doing. I called those years the "maintenance years." I was always feeding, wiping, burping, patting or changing a child. Yet, I fell in love with this new tradition of taking my daughters to the beach. Life was already different for my daughters. Vacation would never be a foreign word to them. They would talk to classmates effortlessly and easily about their vacations. In the fall of school year, they would be able to write essays about the exciting trips on summer break. Amber and Celeste took to the beach differently, however. Amber was a fat golden Buddha baby and she would love to plunk her chunky self down in the sand and let the waves wash over her rolls. Celeste was another story. This lean Gandhi-looking toddler took one look at the water and began running away, as if the waves were chasing her. Maternally, my instinct was to grab her in the safety of my arms whispering words calming words. Yet, I secretly questioned, from where did this fear stem?

Had I somehow handed down an unspoken premise or fear to my daughter? Or simply was it more logical and rational than that? Was she engaging in what psychology terms the "adaptive unconscious," where she was intimately sizing up her world to denote a perceived danger? Or was she just merely at a developmental stage where she lacked differentiation. Whatever the cause of her fear she had already dipped into the Redmond family belief system. I think some part of me will always believe on a cellular level I had passed this fear down to my daughter like it was passed down to me, a familial legacy. Was I a carrier? Was my daughter also a sensitive seed able to pick up what I radiated? Or was she sensitive to the water and what it emanated? Yet, what I did differently was allow my daughters to take swimming lessons at a very early age.

The majority of blacks do not swim, but those reasons are as complex and complicated. Yet, I surmise the reasons are environment, finances and socialization. Yet, one can look at the historical role of water. Homeopathic science believes that water is capable of retaining "memory." As I was reading *Lose Your Mother* by Saidya Hartman, I came across this passage that slaves were "Often under great apprehension at the sight of the sea" according to the slave captain John Newton, because they imagined they are bought to be eat (sic)." I did not fully understand the horrifics of the Middle Passage until listening to the soundtrack of the *Power of One* in my thirties. The music made a profound impression, I felt I too had been submerged and felt the horrors of the eleven million that never made it to the American shores due to illness, murder and suicide. I do know that Dr. Joy DeGruy Leary pierced a veil with her coining of the phrase, Post Traumatic Slave Syndrome. Much of what many African-Americans suffer occurs from this unacknowledged condition. Healing cannot take place until we unearth the impact of slavery and how it has permeated our culture. Djaloki, an educator and philosopher, informed me on the shores of Haiti that many Haitians built their houses faced away from the ocean because of their turbulent relationship and history with water. The Middle Passage voyage was a betrayal. When I heard this explanation it made perfect spiritual sense. There are many in the black community now who have no reservations of water but still that statistics show according to the Centers for Disease Control, black children and teenagers are 2.3 times more likely to drown than whites in this age group.

I imagine bodies of water beckon too many, and that is why so many people are drawn to the varying shades of green, gray and blue. If one does not dream of water or respite externally or internally, how far does the soul progress? One remains bound to the dry un-inspirational mundane surroundings. As a poet, I began taking forays away from the working world and from my obligations to family to attend writer residencies. I recognized the value of retreat and respite and how it fueled creativity. As a first generation college student I was embarking on many other firsts in my family: The first woman to own a home and the first poet. While at the Vermont Studio Center in Johnson, Vermont, I will never forget the day when several poets, writers and artists decided to go to a swimming hole. It wasn't until we started winding our way in the backwoods of Vermont, that I felt that familiar fear edge up my spine. The swimming hole was on private property. You had to know someone who knew someone to know how to even get there. Again, I was participating in a first but I could not erase the images of Emmet Till and men hanging from trees. Logically and intellectually I knew I would be fine, but again like Myrtle Beach I felt like an interloper and an intruder. The other artists were having true "Mountain Dew Moments"; I however only sat on an outcropping of rocks, dipped my toes and thought about how far I had come from Greenville, South Carolina, but not that far. Around me I still carried a blanket of my parents making. I felt like I shed some of the fear but only incrementally within me I carried the scars and turmoil of the red clay land. It did not matter whether I was in Vermont or the Carolinas the wounds were calling out to be soothed and healed.

On the way back I realized I had never been to a swimming hole because one would have to be a landowner for that to occur. I thought about all the ramifications of owning land, wealth, stability and security. In the *New York Times* article, "Forty Acres and a Gap in Wealth," Henry Louis Gates reports,

> I have been studying the family trees of 20 successful African-Americans, people in fields ranging from entertainment and sports (Oprah Winfrey, the track star Jackie Joyner-Kersee) to space travel and medicine (the astronaut Mae Jemison and Ben Carson, a pediatric neurosurgeon). And I've seen an astonishing pattern: 15 of the 20 descend from at least one line of former slaves who managed to obtain property by 1920 — a time when only 25 percent of all African-American families owned property.

Gates theorizes,

> If the correlation between land ownership and success of African-Americans argues that the chasm between classes in the black community is partly the result of social forces set in motion by the dismal failure of 40 acres and a mule, then we must act decisively. If we do not, ours will be remembered as the generation that presided over a permanent class divide, a slow but inevitable process that began with the failure to give property to the people who had once been defined as property.

With pen and paper I try to right the wrongs done unto me and to the collective.

"Unknown Jewels"

> I, descendant of slaves,
> am not ashamed
> the only shame I claim,
> I do not know their names.
> Pouring libations for unknowns
> I refuse to let high school text
> hush history, list content
> that instruct my ways.
> It is said, *those who deliver the punch*
> *soon forget, those who take the hit never forget.*
> We are elegant elephants memories large
> with West African Coast stomps.
> Our music imbued.
> Our song empowered.
> Our dance quickened.
> We, descendants of slaves shimmer
> without shame.

As a poet my life's work has been about strengthening my tribal bonds in order for me to walk more wholly in the world. It is my belief the more secure a person or tribe feels, the more enlivened and enriched, thus giving back and elongating not only the individual lifespan but that of the community. I was forty when I finally made my peace with water. I was ironically in Haiti, a cousin of Africa. I went to work in the orphanages, as well as take a journey to the Memory Village, N a Sonje. The Memory Village is intended to be an interactive historical exercise where people can be immersed in a simulated trans-Atlantic slave trade experience.

One day off the shores Port au Prince, I let it loose to a few of the group members that I was traveling with that I had never floated on my back. Jokingly, I said I have trust and abandonment issues. Yet, within me I knew it to be true. I took me wherever I needed to go but my muscles my whole self had ached to be carried to trust to be led. It was if the universe had conspired to dismantle the fear that I had harbored so long and on the foreign shores of Haiti, the Universe gave me a gift I could not give myself as I faced the deepest precipice on that shore I found myself strangely facing my fear of water, by doing what my mother had always warned me about, doing nothing all along — all I had to do was be me and go with the flow but first I had had to trust.

"The Way of Water"

I have never floated before
never laid back because fear
slept quietly under my pillow.
on the shores of Haiti women arms cradled me
rocking me with the waves of knowledge the ocean is a woman, Erzulie
A seven woman strong circle
tenderly surrounded me upon that ancient bed of blue
they let me go from arms to hands to fingertips
until I grew from baby to child to toddler to woman.
I float on my own flat back as feminine seas rock me.
I float for the first time on fluid forgiveness.
I float for all the times I never knew the world
would and could come up to meet me
touch me with gentleness.
Wash over me with unforeseen kindness
The sun overhead trust becomes an orange globe
growing inside warming.
I am armed no more with the clenching of teeth
the cinching of muscle
the waves say let go
on the rocking rhythm I float
I become a knowing boat
that belief and faith are healers
and sometimes you have to lay back
let trust cup you like water
and carry you effortlessly home.

Black Power

by STEPHANIE POWELL WATTS

The Lackey twins sat across from me on the school bus. I hated the twins. Stuck on each other like cockleburs. Rich, crybaby faces always taking up the special air in the room. The twins needed a break, the twins are scared, the twins are sad or crying or annoyed. Again. Unfortunately for me, it was the mid-seventies in rural North Carolina and the Lackey twins and I were the three black kids in my class at West Lenoir Elementary School. This meant (no discussion) me and the Lackey twins were friends.

Not that I lacked for white chums. There was Allison, an only child and lucky enough to have television in her room *and* in her daddy's van. Sweet, big-eyed Julie, who made noise in inverse proportion to her tiny little frame. Julie, who had a record player and a personal record collection. I had to replace her Paul McCartney and Wings 45 after one weekend when I spent the better part of the waking days memorizing the words to "Silly Love Songs" (words I know still). I rocked that 45 and sprung up like an arrow when the singing ended and the needle hit those silent grooves at the end. The second I heard that static-y bump, bump, bump like a heart murmur in the room, I was ready to play that song one more time. Turns out that if you pick up a record needle over a hundred fifty times in a row (roughly the life of the record), you are bound to scratch the surface, making Paul McCartney's seventies smooth sound like old school rap. What's wrong with that? What's — What — What's wrong with that? What's wrong — wrong — wrong — wrong with that?

In those days, there was always music in my house. Daddy's upstairs taste ran to Ray, Goodman and Brown, Stevie Wonder, Harold Melvin, Melba Moore, perfect soul harmonies that, if they were food, would be more like warm caramel than the bubble gum I loved. But the basement was a more complicated story. I knew Daddy had his secrets. I knew when he thought nobody saw, he sneaked some Carpenters on the 8-track down there. He's my father, I don't judge him. Besides, it was the seventies. It was a different time.

But of all of my white friends, I loved Donna best. Beautiful Donna whose big elementary school teeth were coming in straight. Donna, with the long dark hair that waved expectantly in anticipation of the Eighties manes we would all wear. Donna, my favorite, who even years later after my mother left my father and dropped Lenoir, North Carolina, like it was scalding to the tongue, sent me a news clipping about the death of her elementary school crush, Jim Beall. A clipping I was sure I'd keep forever. I had plenty of friends. But it was only the Lackey twins that had to make the trip with me to get inoculated for sickle cell anemia.

Every black kid in Caldwell County was required to get the inoculation that just might save our lives. In a post–AIDS epidemic world, it is hard to believe that people quaked in fear about this relatively small-scale disease, but we did. We were scared. Few of us had seen, but we'd all heard about the television movie with the beautiful black woman, Cicely Tyson or some other luminary. Her halo of afro diffusing the moonlight, the dashing fiancé at her side, both with desk jobs. But wait, the beautiful black woman contracted sickle cell, died tragically young and all the dreams of this budding black family, *poof!*, up in smoke. Slavery, Jim Crow, Hidden Crow, and now sickle cell. When would we catch a break? We were all raised better than to believe that everything would turn out fine. So when the school said that all of us had to get our shots, we went. Nobody worried too much about it. Crazy as it sounds to me now, none of us talked conspiracy. Nobody's parents caused a ruckus and complained about tainted medicine or rigged brakes on our ancient school buses. Even the twins' parents with their two-car garage, cloth napkins, matching bedspreads and curtains put them on the bus like the rest of us. Our fear was more personal, even primal. This wasn't about white people, but the betrayal of our own black bodies, our own sweet little cells mowing us down in our primes.

The buses took us to a black community called Freedman (no kidding) to the Recreation Center there. The rec was on a hill, off the main street of the community, surrounded by tulip poplars and scrubby pines. I'd been to the rec plenty of times, especially during the summer when my father held softball tournaments and my brothers and I played with the other kids on any empty field available or in the rooms in the main facility until somebody ran us out. To the right of the rec center stood two rickety frame houses, rented by people Daddy always stopped to wave to. The only other building you could see from the parking lot was Freedman High School, the old all-black high school, closed and abandoned for years.

Drive down the hill into the tiny valley, the old brick, building looked like some afterthought, too small for any high school these days. I'd never been in the school, but years before, Daddy took my four brothers and me to wander around outside. "There must be the lunch room, there the library," Daddy said and pointed at cracked and broken windows as we circled through the weeds around the building. He added a few good time stories that we didn't care about or understand. All his yarns were bittersweet with punch lines that made segregation sound like a bona-fide lark.

Daddy had been a football player, a star to hear him tell it. That was all well and good, but I loved the stories his younger sister, my Aunt Candy, told about being a Blue Imp cheerleader. She'd demonstrate her technique in my yard, dragging a chair from our kitchen to rest on in between cheers, kick off her clogs (in my mind she is always in clogs — shoes I forever associate with insouciance), her bare feet disappeared in the grass. I'd sit on some bad spot in the shade where Daddy had given up on grass taking root, away from the border of yellow four o'clocks and marigolds, my back to the still half-finished barbeque pit. What used to promise barbeques is now a trash burning pit, but then it was reaching upwards, a beckoning to good times just two, no more than three mortar lines away.

"We're the Blue Imps," Candy said, her hand cocked on a hip. "And we're slick and fine," she pivoted on her invisible feet, her full lips pouted. "If you mess with us, we will blow your mind." Candy recited cheer after cheer, each one ending in violence or a threat, "My name is Candy. That's no lie. You mess with me. I'll black your eye." Candy told me to teach the cheers to my girlfriends at school. My parents knew by name, at least the family name, every black person in town. They all went to the same parties in basements that looked like ours with Coleman beer coolers in the corner and off to the side a fold-up table where the pickled sausage and feet, chips, dips and party mints sat in a damp corner. I'm sure Candy imagined me surrounded by my eager black friends, all waiting for an infusion of soul old-school style and not the pale little girls I knew, their eyes bulging and fearful if I showed them how we do.

I don't remember too many specifics about that day. I know Todd Banner was there, because I hated the lecherous way he looked at me. Me, a piss-ass child, nobody's woman with a skinny little body and flat chest, long pigtails that I had to force myself not to twirl around my fingers when I was nervous. I know Mrs. Ingram wasn't there. She was a teacher in another county, the first and only black teacher I had in twelve years of public school. I loved her hard. Everything about her I drank in and memorized. Her thin set mouth, the dark gap between her teeth, her exasperated sigh when the boys in the class did something disgusting. "Yes, you can," she'd insist even if you hadn't protested, even if you'd done your best to show no fear.

What I do remember are the kids. Busload after busload of black kids from the elementary, middle and high schools, brown, black, every shape and size. More black kids than I had ever seen in my life. I tried to count us all: Parks, Alexanders, Hightowers, Banners, Dulas, Hoods, Chapmans, Johnsons, Michaux, Watkins, Powells, Thomases. Black kids everywhere. A whole generation of us in one place. I lived in a black neighborhood and every Sunday, my parents would take us to the loud, congested house of my grandparents where by evening the adults lingered on the porch watching the children, burning rags to keep away the mosquitoes and if my grandmother would allow it, blasting funk from the soul station out of Charlotte, North Carolina into the dark. I was not unaccustomed to seeing black faces. Still, this meeting of all of us, the sheer numbers of young people, all in this one place and one time, made me inexplicably proud.

Today I am one of a small number of black professors at a private university. I don't live in a black neighborhood anymore and most of my friends are the people I went to graduate school with and work with at the college. Most of them are white. There's nothing wrong with any of that. That's not my point. What I find remarkable is that after all this time, I understand what my father felt when we returned to Freedman High. I know why he wanted us to see it with him, though nothing of its vitality remained. It has taken me more than twenty-five years, but I see now the enormous power in togetherness. Coming together, even in pain or because of the threat of pain, is still together. I don't regret a lot, but if I had to do it over, I would have tapped the twins on the shoulder that day. I would have said in the ways that children do that we were all afraid. I would spread out my hands at the sight before the three of us and say something like, "Look at us. Can you believe it?" I would teach them the chant my Aunt Candy taught me. The chant I loved above all the others: *Ungawa, ungawa, black power, black power.* I wouldn't have taken the moment for granted if I'd had any idea how beautiful and ephemeral it would ultimately turn out to be.

1987 Tenth Grade

by CAMIKA C. SPENCER

Going into seventh grade I was uprooted from urban school life. The year was 1987. Until then, my elementary school surroundings were Black. All of my friends were Black. We celebrated Black History Week, and community was in place. My color was not an issue and never had been until then. Having to go to a school with White small-town kids both frightened and excited me. Attending Lancaster would bring my Blackness to the surface. Lancaster, a suburb of Dallas, had its own ruling body, school system, grocery stores and banks and was run and regulated by the all-White City Council. Lancaster was a place where mostly Caucasians lived, and for my mother it was the bittersweet punishment.

My brother Tony, who is two years older than me, attended South Oak Cliff in Dallas as a freshman. South Oak Cliff was an all-Black high school in Dallas that had a falling reputation, but nothing my mother felt she had to worry about. My brothers and I were good, obedient kids. However, in 1986 during his final ninth-grade semester, my mother discovered upon receiving his report card that Tony had flunked his Algebra class due to lack of attendance. He'd skipped the entire semester, ashamed because he was a freshman in a class full of seniors. My mother was furious, and she went to the school and gave the office staff a verbal lashing; I'm sure the office workers on duty that day still talk about it. She was upset that nobody had called her to let her know that her son was not coming to school. She didn't grow up in "that kind" of educational environment, and her kids weren't the kind of kids not to show up for days at a time. My mother is old school, and she comes from old school ways. The days when boys still courted girls, kids still slow danced, and adults made sure children didn't misbehave without immediate action.

Until seventh grade, I was being raised by my community with my mother's help. She'd been thinking about it for some time because according to her, "The schools aren't like they used to be." To her, this meant that people cared about the students because the students had parents "who cared." The community raised the kids at various levels and parents were held accountable. So it was settled. My brothers and I were being sent to "that White school out in Lancaster, since we didn't know how to behave in a regular school."

I would spend my next three-and-a-half years coming of age in two worlds: the solidly middle-class Black subdivision of Singing Hills in the Oak Cliff section of Dallas and the solidly middle-class White suburban town of Lancaster. My parents had gotten divorced, and my father had recently bought a house in Lancaster, a city of roughly sixteen-thousand that is south of Dallas. We were to use our father's address there while living with my mother in Singing Hills. My brothers were purchased a car for us to make the fifteen-mile trek, crossing the city limit twice a day, five days a week, and that's all she wrote. I still lived an urban life overall and basically never had to be around or deal with White people, in the name of a more informed education process on behalf of my mother. She was trying not to turn her back on the Black experience in education, but she felt it had failed her.

I enjoyed Lancaster once I settled in. The kids were pretty segregated during that first year, but by my tenth grade year in 1987, there was open interracial dating, Hispanic students had begun to make more of a presence, and the faces of the staff and faculty were beginning to change. My teachers were no longer all Caucasian. However, I always knew it as a country White school — not racist, just country and Caucasian. My first year, I spent a lot of time not being recognized, just tolerated. I spent a lot of time being funny, but not taken seriously. I spent a lot of time listening to and documenting the things I was hearing and experiencing. My mother made it clear that we were there to get into our education, not get into fights. Blacks still had to depend heavily on numbers, and Lancaster was a challenge, but I enjoyed my time there — that is, until tenth grade.

I was expelled from the athletics program at Lancaster, because the head coach of the track program pushed me one morning. He yelled that I wasn't running fast enough. He called me a quitter. I told him to fuck himself and ran out the gym in tears. The next thing I knew, my volleyball coach and her assistant were telling me I wouldn't play sports at Lancaster again. But volleyball season was over, and that's all that mattered to me — I'd finished the season on a good note, and I was moving, so my days were numbered anyway. Still, I was not prepared for what I was about to experience.

After Christmas break, my dad moved from Lancaster, my mother re-married, and my step-dad's job was moving them to Hagerstown, Maryland. I had to transfer to a Dallas school for a total of three months, and I dreaded it. The traditional high schools where Blacks once kept up, acted well and learned had gained bad and dwindling reputations. Now, without my father living in Lancaster, I couldn't finish sophomore year with friends, like Toni Patterson. Toni was my best friend at Lancaster. She was Black and loved Prince. I think I introduced her to the music of Too Short. And my crush at Lancaster that year was Johnny Tatum, a senior, and Toni's crush was a junior named Michael Benson. Both guys were blacker than night itself and nothing at all like the light-skinned guys we dreamed about having that summer before but never got around to getting. We had crushes on a few of the white boys, too, but nothing that was ever taken past mere conversation.

I kept feeling the tears stinging my eyes, because I couldn't remain at Lancaster, and my only stop was South Oak Cliff High School — the same place that had allowed my brother to skip a single class for six-weeks. On the street it was now referred to as either the School of Crime or Skip Out Class. I was terrified and had to ride home listening to my father talk about how sorry he was about the research *my mother* had failed to do and how I would just have to bite the bullet and make the best of it.

My mother dropped me off at South Oak Cliff the morning of new enrollment. She must have figured that, since I lived in the district, all I needed to do was sign up for classes, because she left me on the curb with enough cash to get lunch and told me to catch the bus home. She didn't walk me to the door. She didn't make sure I talked to the right people. In the main office, there were people everywhere. The place was total chaos. There were bodies crowding the desk and bodies in all five of the waiting chairs, and the walking space in between was a constant trail of foot traffic coming and going. Women, kids and teens, mostly. The secretary was being barraged with questions and requests for everything from schedule changes and tardy passes to enrollments, and even by one student trying to get back into school after being thrown out. Some people seemed to just be visiting friends. Then, there was me — taking it all in — standing at the counter trying to get the secretary to notice me.

Finally, she peered in my direction and said, "Baby, what do you want?" She sounded like she had been there all day and that I was the last person she wanted to see, when it was the start of her work day and we'd never met before. She was a dark woman. A weary-looking woman with a lot of yell stored up inside her meaty build. Her glasses had gold-plated chain holders dangling from the sides, and she was chewing gum with her lips tightly closed. I told her that I was there to enroll. She told me I was in the wrong office. I was to go to the guidance office. She immediately walked away to handle another cause at the other end of the counter. Where in the hell was the guidance office? Figuring this was hell, I knew it had to be somewhere in the building, so I left the office and stood for a second to get my bearings. This guy walked by and I immediately asked, but he didn't know either — answered with a mutter and a shrug. I looked above doors as I walked the hall end-to-end, totally unable to find the guidance office.

The halls of South Oak Cliff were old, and the school lacked the updated lockers and technology and brightness that I experienced at Lancaster. Tiles were missing from the hall floors, and not all of the ceiling lights were lit. Kids either looked past me or not at all. Kids at Lancaster were friendly. There were so few of us who were Black that, unless you had beef, you spoke to each other. I stopped and looked at the dozen or so antiquated senior class photos posted in a case at the end of one hall and learned that between 1965 and 1970, the student body changed from nearly 100 percent white to almost 100 percent African-American as South Oak Cliff went through a period of rapid change demographically. Being born in 1971, I had never known a *white* South Oak Cliff High School. Now, I was walking the halls of this school amongst my own people, not wanting to get shot, robbed, or knocked up. I didn't have these types of thoughts or concerns at Lancaster where a part of me feels I should have. Sure, I wasn't excited about possibly being called a nigger, but I was prepared to handle that on all fronts. Black-on-Black crime is another beast entirely. Things had changed drastically in less than fifteen years for South Oak Cliff. My grandfather said that the Whites had left and taken their money with them and then didn't allow the Black man to flourish. However, I knew that having nice things had little to do with money and more to do with the action of caretaking. You don't need money to have nice things. You need effort and generosity, and South Oak Cliff wasn't getting much generosity or effort. It was a school where I could tell few people cared.

The halls were quiet and empty on that first day. I began to get frustrated and was copping an attitude when an old friend from elementary, Yvette Lewis, emerged from behind one of the hallway doors. We had been close in grade school and lived in the same neighborhood, around the corner from each other, until I moved away to Singing Hills twelve miles away and began attending school in the Lancaster district. Actually, I'd known Yvette since nursery. I'd forgotten she'd attended SOC until I saw her. We hugged, and after finding out I was trying to enroll, she took me to the guidance office, which was behind the door she had emerged from. The door with no room number nor label. Yvette was an aide in there during one of her class periods. She told me most of the students don't come to school until like the second week of school, hence the quite halls and few people to guide me.

The guidance office was small with green painted walls, three office rooms and a waiting area. There was a desk and a few tables for the aides to sit and put their books. I gave the secretary my name and told her why I was there. She asked me if had I gotten my enrollment card from the main office. I didn't have the card, so I knew that I would have to go back to the chaos.

I headed back to the main office, swallowing hard to deal with the secretary's blank stares, and the chaos. The office was as chaotic as ever. This time, the tired secretary noticed me right off.

"Baby, you back in here already?"

"Uh, the lady in guidance told me to get a pink enrollment card." I saw the cards at the edge of the counter, picked one up and started to walk out.

"Hold on." She crossed her arms. "Is your parent here?"

"Not in here with me, ma'am. No."

She held her hand out and gave me the 'give it here' gesture. "Baby, you can't have one of these unless your parent is here to fill it out."

I stood there watching the secretary put the pink card on top of the others that were stacked at the end of the counter. She walked off after rolling her eyes at me and telling me to go home and stop wasting her time. She started talking to some guy at the other end of the counter, away from the stack of enrollment cards, who was begging her to let him back in school.

Certain that my mother was stuck in morning traffic by now on her forty-five minute commute to her job, and not wanting to deal with my father — for to do that was to have to listen to how all this was my mother's fault — I made myself determined to get enrolled at least. I began to move toward the end of the counter. I was praying that this guy along with the others would keep her attention. She turned her back to look up a phone number for the kid begging to get back into school. I buried myself into the crowd of office visitors and took a card. Then, I hurried into the hall and forged my mom's name. I had to get into SOC before the day was over, or else I would chicken out and never go back. I took the card back to guidance and got closer to enrollment.

Turning in the card placed me on a first-come-first-served waiting list to see the P-5 guidance counselor. When she called, "Next," nobody moved so I jumped up and went in. The counselor was sort of short with fair skin and a black curly wig. She reminded me of a lady who might run a candy store from her garage or from the kitchen table in a small apartment. She asked me lots of questions, like what kind of academic background I had, had I played sports, and when was my birth date. Don't get the idea that she was trying to make me more comfortable or to relax me. She was like the lady in the main office, but with a little more patience. She scared me, however, talking at me instead of to me and looking me up and down. She called Lancaster to find out how soon she could get a copy of my transcript. That's when the lunch bell rang. She got up and told me to come back after lunch. If Lancaster didn't call back, I would have to wait until they did call before my complete enrollment could go through.

So here I was nervous and paranoid. I wasn't comfortable leaving the guidance office, so I just sat in the waiting area until my counselor came back. When she returned, she had a note that Lancaster had called but that they would have to mail my transcripts. The guidance counselor went ahead and enrolled me anyway.

Being inside a school that carried a bad reputation in a Black neighborhood wasn't as bad as I imagined. The atmosphere was more laid back than at Lancaster, and as long as I went to my classes and didn't gravitate towards trouble, I was good. I liked all of my teachers there.

I think my meanest teacher was Mrs. Carlita Newsom. She taught choir and called me "Baby," as she looked at me trying to remember my name. She was a big woman and liked loud soul-filled voices. I was a bother to her — light in voice, but obedient and respectful. I stayed quiet in her room, because when she was having a good day, we couldn't tell unless she laughed, which was rare. She couldn't sing very well either — just loud — but her piano playing and teaching techniques more than made up for her vocal weakness.

Choir was my second favorite class, composed of mostly seniors who kept it exciting for me that year. I remember a few of them: Latricia was the fashion plate, guaranteed to have the latest hairstyle and to be dressed from head to toe is something designer. She wore make-up and emitted cool from her being. Walter was big and soft. A smart-looking boy with a lot of book sense and crazy light-brown eyes embedded in a baby face the color of camel fur. Vincent was the athlete and the one who had to be asked to keep his feet off the desks and to put his gum in the trash. Shannon was the preachers' son about my skin color. His father's church was in my neighborhood, not far from my house.

Mr. Sims' biology class was not normal at all. Mr. Sims was a widower. His wife was killed in an auto accident and since then he never drove. He rode the city transportation to work. His tone of voice lacked any emotion, but it was full of wisdom.

My favorite class at the School of Crime was Study Hall. Mrs. Gillespie was the teacher. All she did was sit at her desk, read the paper, sleep, gossip, or sell candy — whichever came first. Mrs. Gillespie never said very much, but when she did, she got her point across. The kids liked her. I thought she was lazy, but she was a cool lady for giving us a break in the day.

My homemaking class was led by Mrs. Gomez. She was a Mexican-American who spoke both English and Spanish fluently. There was one Mexican girl at the school who would stop by our class and speak Spanish with Mrs. Gomez almost every morning. Our class would mimic them by making noises as if we were speaking it too. I love it. This guy named Quincy Dayton, who was in homemaking with me, took an admirer's liking to me. The feeling wasn't mutual. He was heavy set with the fattest close-cut-carrying head on anyone I knew. He talked slow and had a gold cap on one of his front teeth. He also loved to cheat. I almost hated him because he bugged me constantly about hooking up.

Another class was Government with Mr. Ackerman, a short, white, fragile-looking white man who seemed nervous all the time. To let him tell it, he accidentally signed up for teaching in a lower-income area. It was *all* an accident. Mr. Ackerman had right to be nervous, because the majority of this class was repeaters. The fun bunch was in there. I laughed constantly in this class. I don't remember much about Mr. Ackerman except he was white and should not have been teaching at SOC. I felt sorry for him even more than I felt for myself.

My English teacher was Ms. Novak. She was white also, but a lot more conscious about her situation and what went on around her. She had a son that was attending another DISD school in another district. I never felt sorry for Ms. Novak, because she would defend herself.

My last class was Algebra I. My teacher was Mrs. Delaney. She had the greatest hair too. Mrs. Delaney had smooth coconut-colored skin, and referred to all of her students as "Sweet Baby." She would say things like, "Go to the board and work the problem, Sweet Baby," or "Sweet Baby, get into this classroom." She was relatable. She also had dark lips and I often wondered if she smoked.

After school, I rode bus #919. It made two trips, and people rarely caught the first bus out. I scrambled to make that first bus each day. The quiet bus where I usually got my own seat. The second load ran late and catching it meant possibly having no seat at all. The people on second load were rowdy. I can't remember a dull time riding home on second load when I did. There were several fights, always a good game of the dozens going down, and some girl was constantly getting felt up by the roguish boys that caught the bus. They called the bus driver "Busee." He was a man in about his mid-fifties who never let too much bother him. He also never said much, just things like "Sit down," or "Don't throw things out my window." But he never put in any power behind his voice. He survived that way so I guess it worked for the best.

Once during an early release day, Busee wasn't driving and a substitute driver, an African man, was in place and he was making only one trip. The bus was crowded and this African bus driver got off to a bad start by telling everybody to sit down and shut up or he wasn't leaving the parking lot. A few kids on the bus started chanting, "Bullshit." One kid, who was full of one-liners and eager to be the comedian, yelled that he was going to take the bus driver to court. This made the bus erupt in laughter. I was growing more afraid in my following as things progressed. Finally, the bus driver pulled out of the parking lot and got underway. The usual fanfare of having too many kids on a bus began. The dozens, hands going where they have no business, loud talking, item throwing and candy eating. Two boys, Luther and Eric, began rough-housing which made the bus driver pull over and begin yelling at us all to get off his bus. He opened the doors and pointed us all toward the exit. I wanted to get up, but was window-seated next to a girl who wasn't budging. Kids were laughing again, not threatened, not obeying the orders to evacuate the bus, just laughing. The bus driver felt a need to start preaching at us for the next three minutes or so. Then, this short kid named Andre yelled out the unthinkable. "Shut up, Kunta!" The bus rocked with the mass hysteria of laughter. The bus driver bounded down the aisle and tried to find out who said it. This made him more determined to put everyone off the bus. Since the bus was not far from my street, I excused myself and got off. I felt sorry for that bus driver and embarrassed how he'd been treated. This was just one of the stunts. I remember fights in the halls, kids jumping from windows to ditch class, and kids cussing teachers. SOC lived up to its reputation, but there were more great, talented, good-natured Black kids there than rumored.

When school ended that year, I was glad. I left SOC, eager for the next challenge of attending my junior year in another state in another part of the country. I didn't know what to expect from the kids or the community at South Hagerstown, but I Lancaster all but prepared me to deal with the white folk, and South Oak Cliff helped me to deal with the Black, and nothing to follow could be better or worse.

Why It Matters

by ANNE ESTEPP

When I was five years old, I came home from kindergarten and taught my sister a new word game I had learned from one of the boys in my class. It was actually a variation on a word game I had played with my cousins for years: "eeny, meeny, miney, moe, catch a tiger by the toe." The new variation I had been taught, replaced "tiger" with "nigger." I had no clue what that word meant, but as soon as my parents heard it escape my lips, my mama slapped me on the mouth with the flat of her hand, as though she could slap the word back through my lips and teeth where it would stay locked and never come out again. As she and my daddy later explained, "nigger" was a curse word, the same as "shit" and "damn," and no self-respecting Christian person would ever use that word. To me it was just a word. Being from the mountains of eastern Kentucky I had never seen an African American in my life, let alone a "nigger."

My parents never talked about race. My father had grown up dirt-poor and like many young men in eastern Kentucky, he fled the mountains for the factories in Michigan. Working at General Motors during the 1960s, he labored alongside African Americans, but he never talked about it with my sisters and me. Growing up in an all-white, lower-class community during the 1980s my first contact with African Americans was through the television. "The Cosby Show" was my favorite sitcom and I would often find myself wishing that Claire and Heathcliffe Huxtable were my parents. I didn't care that they were black. He was a doctor, she a lawyer, and they lived the upper-middle class-brownstone-New York City-kind of life that the dreary backdrop of a coal-mining town failed to offer. As a teenager during the early 1990s, my friends and I became enamored with the gang-ster rap craze that swept the nation when Dr. Dre, Snoop Dog, and Tupac took over the MTV airwaves. (A sure sign that pop culture has no color if there ever was one.) We had no concept of what they were rapping about, we just thought it was "cool." I don't believe that I ever connected injustice with race until later when the Los Angeles race riots in 1992 and the OJ Simpson trial in 1995 seemingly consumed every minute of the news. The image of the LAPD beating on Rodney King, the acquittal of his attackers, and the ensuing riots, flipped a switch in my consciousness. I began to realize that there was a divide between Americans over race that I had never noticed. I became aware of the fact that I had spent my life in a bubble. When you grow up around only one race, class distinctions become so defined, so cemented, that things like race become irrelevant. In a sense, you believe that race doesn't matter.

I moved to Alabama in 2002 to pursue my doctorate in history at Auburn University. During my second year of coursework I took a class on modern Appalachian history. It was in this class that I learned more about the labor struggles in the Kentucky coal-fields. Growing up fifteen minutes from "bloody" Harlan, I knew all about United Mine Workers leader John Lewis and the brutality of the coal-mine operators whose harsh tactics in breaking up strikes had earned the town its nickname. I also had first-hand knowledge of the perilous working conditions in the mines since the vast majority of men in my family worked or had worked in the mines at some point. What I did not know was that, during those strikes, African Americans were used as scabs to replace striking miners and that a small number of those men and their families remained in Harlan. This wouldn't have been such a shock if my father's ancestral heritage wasn't such a mystery.

My father and his siblings were blessed with wavy, ink-black hair, dark eyes, and very dark skin, features they explained away as "Indian blood"—despite the fact that Native Americans had not lived in our part of Kentucky for two hundred years. When I asked my father if it were possible that his grandmother (who had never known who her father was) might have been part African-American I was met with incredulity, anger, and downright denial.

Over the years I have pressed my father to have a DNA test to determine his heritage and every time he refuses. And my mother agrees with him. I realized my parents who had never talked about race and insisted that "nigger" was a curse word, would rather *believe* my father to be Native American, and thus my sisters and I as well, than to know his real ancestry. That's when I realized that even in my hometown, where everyone is white, race matters. It's just that no one wants it to matter because that makes thing too difficult; it opens a new can of worms. It is easier to look down upon your shiftless white neighbor who hasn't had a job in ten years and draws welfare because that somehow makes sense. Race is too abstract, too inconceivable, and at the end of the day, too disturbing.

In reference to slavery, Thomas Jefferson once said, "We have the wolf by the ears, and we can neither hold him, nor safely let him go." Slavery no longer exists, but race is still the wolf that Jefferson spoke of. I've found in Alabama, race is something everyone is aware of— it's the wolf at your door that you can't possible ignore. It is strong and powerful and it is not going away. In my tiny, homogenous world tucked away in the hills of Kentucky, race is more like a kitten meowing at your door: you either let it in, or ignore it and hope it goes away. The best you can hope for is that it will leave you alone and someone else will take care of it.

The Difference

by ASHLEY DAY

As children of the 1970s in south Alabama, my brother and I grew up surrounded by extended family. My parents were born in the late 1940s in small Mississippi towns but reared in the big city of Mobile (or at least its outskirts) by women determined to leave swept-dirt front yards behind. Their people — my people — were sawmill workers, dirt farmers, horse traders, and shade-tree mechanics. They raised much of their own food, made most of their own clothes, fixed their own cars, and often built their own modest homes. It is from this rural, working-class white world my parents sprung.

On Mama's side, the Gibsons are my grandparents, five aunts, their seemingly irrelevant husbands, and well over a dozen cousins, of which I am the eldest. Childhood summers were spent visiting at one aunt's house or another, engaging in one of three activities: attending vacation bible school, bringing in vegetables and preparing them for canning or freezing, or roaming the countryside with my cousins. A pack of children sent out to play after breakfast, we were expected to look out for each other, not act ugly or get ourselves hurt, and, most importantly, stay gone until dinner when a plate of sandwiches and pitcher of Kool-Aid would be waiting on the porch. Going in and out of the house was frowned upon, what with the bought air getting out every time the door opened. We gorged on wild huckleberries, plums, and blackberries, tried to avoid yellow jackets and snakes, swam in creeks, climbed trees, played house, poked sticks in ant hills, convinced James to pee on an electric fence, and taunted a bull until he charged. We were barefoot, brown from the dirt and the sun, as free as children today seem corralled.

Daddy was an only child and not particularly close to his extended family, but I was devoted to my grandparents on his side, particularly his mother, who remains my fiercest advocate. She grew up in the country

with an outhouse and a daddy who rolled his own cigarettes on the front
porch using the four remaining fingers on his right hand. For several years
during elementary school I blissfully spent alternate weekends in the suburban tract house she has risen to, cosseted amid heavy drapes and thick
swirled carpet. Coloring books, Sugar Corn Pops, and cartoons were just
three things frowned upon by my parents that I reveled in on these visits.
We went fishing at the river and took trips to the A&P where I always got
a quarter for the gum machine on the way out. I ate Swanson chicken pot
pies and vanilla pudding cups at a plastic-covered dining room table, seated
on an upside down double boiler to make me tall enough. Every September
we watched "The Wizard of Oz" on television, and I always cried when
Dorothy opened the door to Oz, a dizzying world of color, a place so
much richer than black and white.

Alabama was a far cry from California's hippies and their Summer of
Love, but my parents were absolutely children of the 1960s. Their high
schools were integrated while they were in attendance, they believed the
Vietnam War to be unjust and their government to be distrusted, and they
were DIY out of principle as well as financial necessity, whether that meant
growing some of their own food or making yogurt or fixing cars or building
tree houses.

But they were also children of the South with its sense of family,
place, and faith. In an interview with Tom Brokaw about the 1960s, Bruce
Springsteen, whose *Born to Run* is the soundtrack of my childhood, said,
"I found one leg rooted in the place that I came from and another leg
reaching out for the rest of a world that I felt like I needed and wanted."
This in-betweenness, this insider-outsider experience encapsulates my parents' young adulthood and has everything to do with how they chose to
raise their children.

The leg rooted in the past led them to marry in their early twenties
and start a family while enrolled in the local state university, the first people
in either of their families to pursue a college education. While children
were to be celebrated, the value of higher education was questionable. My
maternal grandmother once told Mama, when things between her and
Daddy were bad, that she'd never had such problems "until you started
reading all them books." Mama went on to become a schoolteacher and
Daddy a state administrator, ushering us into the middle class.

In 1971 I was born, followed eighteen months later by my brother.
We lived in married student housing back behind the university in an un-
air-conditioned small brick house with a garden plot where the driveway
ended, deep in a neighborhood that was both black and white. My brother

and I were raised by our extended family and then later bussed to our public elementary school in an effort to maintain integration. I just thought long rides in a yellow school bus were part and parcel of being big enough to go to school.

Race was all around us but it was never discussed. Yet my parents did something that made us stand out from our cousins — they refused to allow the N-word.

When asked about it now, they don't recall any deep discussions, any conscious decision-making. In their minds we simply were no better or worse than anyone else in the world and name-calling was ugly and low-class. They don't and didn't think of banning that word as some sort of revolutionary or evolutionary act. But it was. It set me apart from my cousins and white classmates, put me in a defensive position, made me aware of otherness and how words shape our perception of the world and our place in it at a very young age.

My attentiveness to issues of race, gender, and class — and the inter-sections therein — was born of this single decision. Not using what was then a common enough word among the white folks in my life and intu-iting the *why* is at the core of my ability, many years later, when I was a young college student, to extend the logic to determine how I should treat the first Catholics, gay people, and international students I'd ever come to know.

In 1992 I left Alabama for Atlanta and later New York City. On a recent weekend I sat in my neighborhood playground in Bedford-Stuyvesant talking about the presidential election, an election in which the realities of race and gender have been ever present, and in an attempt to tell a story, I described my brother in part to my brown neighbors as "very straight and very white." One woman tilted her head and not unkindly said, "What are you?" I nearly said, "I'm good white people," how a friend's African-American neighbors described her many years ago, but that was a bucket of worms I didn't need to be digging into. In the end, I was reduced to describing who I am not — I described Mark with his wife, 2.3 kids, suburban home, corporate job, station wagon and truck, chocolate lab, and literal picket fence. He is the white American dream and I am ... not.

In that "not" a gulf exists that I can't seem to cross despite my love and respect for him. For all that we shared growing up together amid the same parents, homes, and schools we are fundamentally separated/lost/dis-tant/apart because I am a white woman who lives, with intention and per-mission, in a brown world. Observing and examining race, gender, class and their intersections is as fundamental to me as a cup of hot coffee in the morning. When I look at the history of my family's rise into the middle class, I see the value of a college education and hard work, but I also see the VA loans that allowed my grandfathers to own homes. I see good-paying jobs with pensions that were open to whites but closed to blacks. I see public schools that were supplied with the tools and teachers necessary to educate people like my parents who went on to garner student loans that enabled them to economically climb to levels their own parents never dreamed of.

My brother says he is tired of hearing about race and that slavery ended more than a hundred years ago. He insists no one ever gave him anything, not seeing the significance of the health insurance we garnered through our father's state job. He is among rarefied company at work, selected for a prestigious management program, his executive MBA paid for, his mentoring deep and thorough. I don't ask how many of his colleagues are of color. He supports Barack Obama but complains about the "this black woman at Wal-Mart with a chip on her shoulder" who acts uppity. In a majority Latino state, he lives on a cul-de-sac occupied solely by white people.

His is not the overt racism of the past, nor even the covert racism of recent decades. Instead he has a presumption of non-racism in post-racial United States that I believe is anything but. And me, I see race always, which is also not the answer. We are two children of the Civil Rights Movement on opposite poles when surely, as in most things, balance is to be found in the middle.

Hed: The Unwritten Rules

by DAWNE SHAND

Mr. Smith serviced my mother's car at his Chevron station in downtown Selma because he always checked the fluids, washed the windshield, and had time to chat. These small additions must have been a comfort to her; they made her reminisce because I can remember hearing her say, as we sat next to each other on the red bench seat, that a team of men used to leap to such tasks. I don't think I could have been more than six. Her '74 Mercury Monarch was temperamental; it stalled on railroad tracks, this I remember well. Often, the wait was for more than a fill-up. Then, my mother would buy, as a treat for me and my sister, a package of salted peanuts and pour a few into a little glass-bottled coke. The half-pieces would swim in the sweet froth. It cut the sugar, she said.

When the car pulled in, it faced a long, squat brick building whose side was covered in fading paint of an advertisement from a different era. "Delicious and Refreshing, Drink Coca-cola, Relieves Fatigue. Sold Everywhere, 5 cents." It already cost a quarter. Weeds grew beneath the sign. Once, from my vantage point of the front window where I sat unbuckled, I read aloud all the words, including fatigue, which I had not yet seen in print. My hair was parted down the middle, hung in two long braids, baby curls framed large brown eyes. I sounded out the large word, "fatigue" with three engorged syllables — fat-eee-guew, I said. Mr. Smith laughed out loud with my mother. Nostalgia and mortification, even three decades later, they seem crisp enough to taste.

Near the sign, a cannonball sat mounted on a plinth to mark the Confederacy's last foundry. Mr. Smith told us the story, I think. The last makers of bullets and cannonballs tossed everything into the river before Selma fell. It was the mid–1970s in Selma, Alabama: the manufacture of Confederate glory was beginning its resurgence. This was the story adults told children, the moment they thought we would find memorable. Four blocks from the Edmund Pettus Bridge, the mud-brown river had become a watery arsenal. Divers even went looking for the treasure.

Once Mr. Smith asked where would I go to school? His question was full of trepidation. "Meadowview," my mother said. She taught at this neighborhood elementary school, the choice public school, where a handful of black students were being bused. I understood there were white schools and black schools, just as I understood the price of a Coke, that the car with the red seats stalled on train tracks, and the river was an arsenal's grave. Simple facts. But the question of my school attendance made me the center of some adult tension that could be felt if not articulated. I cannot recall the muddled codes they used to say the small city couldn't avoid integration past sixth grade. After Meadowview, my mother said to Mr. Smith, "We'll see."

Mr. Smith's white hair stuck out around the edges of his service cap like a monk's tonsure. He turned his head to get a good look at me through the window as my mother paid him. He broke into a wide grin.

"She's going to be a heartbreaker," he said.

At Westside Junior High School, the black girl sitting next to me pulled out a crumpled Polaroid of a baby and claimed it was hers. Could a twelve year old girl, someone my age, have a baby? Her friends began giggling. I shifted nervously, still wide-eyed. Another white girl said to ignore them as a pinched, silver-haired, home-ec teacher demanded quiet while she took roll among the sewing tables. I was twelve, a year away from menstruation. I carried a craft fair lunchbox: my name in red curlicues by a chubby-faced cheerleader with blond pony-tales and pom-poms. On that first morning of seventh grade, I didn't know the answer.

My pigtails were gone. Between orientation and the first day of school, I had my hair cut. My mother had been using the morning hair braiding ritual to upbraid me. A year or two before, the dangers of glue sniffing had been discussed at Meadowview and my mother claimed, as she pulled my hair too taut, I would be locked in a cage for using drugs. Cut free of this routine, freed from her watchful eye and heavy thumb at school, Westside would be exciting. Its band room was full of secret places where we would practice little relationships, called "going together." I stood with a boy between two sets of swinging doors, waiting beneath a broken light to see what darkness would bring. I wrote secrets on pages folded with origami-like care.

In social studies class, my new best friend wrote "I ❤ D²" on my Smurfette folder. We were twelve, studying Mesopotamia, and caught between inchoate sexuality — adoring the androgynous Duran Duran —

and a children's cartoon. This friend joined the small clutch of white girls as we compared skin tones and summer tans. She was so very pretty and part-creole; I half-comprehended that, for the parents, part-creole meant black. Elected to homecoming court, her date to the dance was an effete saxophone player. His father almost disowned him for asking her out, though that knowledge came out (as did he) much later.

The summer between 7th and 8th grade I asked my mother if I could invite this friend to swim at the Marion Junction pool. My mother was sitting on the pool's ledge. By 1982, her vitiligo had progressed to her armpits, knees, and mouth, leaving white blotches on her attractive, olive-tanned skin. Diagnosed years earlier, the disease's destruction of her pigmentation had become her metaphor for teaching that skin color was irrelevant. As a child she'd been asked to write school essays justifying segregation; as an adult, she had joined the public schools and worked toward their integration. She had withdrawn from the Orrville Baptist Church after being asked to justify what she did for the Lord by people she knew were bigots. In protest, she would soon leave an elite professional organization whose membership she had cherished because they refused to hold an award's ceremony anywhere but the segregated Elk's Club. These remarkable, singular stands meant the private swimming pool amid the soybean fields was our last social outlet. My mother said no.

I sobbed in the chlorinated waters. When I lifted my head I caught the last snatch of conversation as my mother said to my sister, "It's the way things are."

The first page of Stendhal's *Charterhouse of Parma* I read in the cafeteria, though we weren't there to eat. Had it been lunch, I wouldn't have been anywhere near the handsome, blond-haired football player; I would have been at the one table of outcast white kids on the black side of the cafeteria. I remember laughing out loud at the elegant language for brothel and that the good-looking junior said something to make me cringe. The high school world was divided between those with sexual knowledge and those without. He was always quick to point out my place.

Some teachers had argued against moving the 9th grad to the high school. Putting 14-years-olds in close contact with the 17- and 18-year-olds would be an inappropriate exposure: they would see their peers smoking in the rear parking lot. The year before, I had been in that first class of 9th graders to join the high school and five months later, stood with all the students in the school's front yard, beneath a crisp January sky, in a moment of silence for the pregnant 14-year-old girl found beaten to death in the basement. The basketball player, whom she had accused at school of being the father, was seventeen, but looked old enough to be tried as an adult for murder.

In French class, we lingered over the choices of Stendhal's main character, Fabrice, who joins Napoleon's army in time to retreat from Waterloo and spends a lifetime asking, "Was I really in the battle?" In our class of precocious readers (one of whom had discovered the dead girl), we would have discussed the irony of Fabrice, a man of the church, meeting his lover in the dark to avoid breaking her vow never to see him. The erotic frustrations of an older century could be discussed and analyzed. The here and now — *they were fourteen and seventeen, she had pulled herself to sitting at a school desk, they were black* — lay engulfed in one, sharp moment of silence.

John had a graceful, measured stride. He walked as if everyone were looking. As he crossed the rear parking lot and a stream of black students left the school — this part of the image remains indelible — his preppy golf shirt emphasized his sculpted chest and arms. He played football and he was a senior. When I pull the memory into focus now I realize how the shirt's pale lemon color flattered his dark skin. We had met in a class called study period, where for thirty minutes after lunch a mix of students had to cool their heels. I always sat by John. Earlier in the winter, he had attempted to introduce me to someone I had a crush on; but, I had been too self conscious. An ugly stocking cap my mother coerced me into wearing had messed the short spikes of my awkwardly cut hair.

It was early summer when band practice ended and I was waiting for my mother to pick me us. John called out. I went to say hello. Perhaps I used one of the stances I'd memorized from the sexy Guess jeans ad in *Seventeen* magazine when I hugged him. That moment, my mother called me to the car. Once I got in, a dress-down ensued. Some things were not done. I had behaved inappropriately. She did not and could not articulate her fears: I had hugged a black man in public, I had broken an unwritten rule.

University of Alabama, 1988. On a September morning a few weeks into my first semester, a professor led the Honors 101 (Introduction to Values) class to a window and asked if we recognized the next door. At that spot twenty-five year earlier, George Wallace had made his infamous "Stand at the Schoolhouse Door," an attempt to uphold his pledge of "Segregation today, segregation tomorrow, segregation forever." For this seminal event in American history, the University had no plaque, no commemoration. It was a sleepy Southern university grown more stringent and self-satisfied with the dull, atmospheric conservatism of Ronald Reagan's America.

I'd started college completely unprepared for the experience of being sought after. During the first weekend, I had been walking back to my dorm with someone I'd just met, a handsome boy as pretty as he was dumb. He'd pulled me suddenly into the vending machine room, pressed me against a wall, kissed me, and unbeknownst to him, walked me across the boundary from adolescent to adult attraction. After class I told him about the schoolhouse door discovery, how little time had passed, how much had changed. "What's the big deal?" the boy from New Orleans feigned.

My mother wanted so badly for me to receive a white mum with silver ribbons for Homecoming that she sent me one herself. At the football game in 1989, a black homecoming queen, having won in a write-in campaign, was crowned on the field as my date's fraternity brothers screamed, "Lynch Her!" Dressed in navy suit jackets and ties, filled with bourbon, the men continued this chant during the half-time ceremonies; it carried across the fraternity section and a Confederate flag waved. I had wanted to be here, wanted to dress in stockings and heels for this tradition, wanted to be included in this society because I knew from high school what it meant to exist on the margins. While I stood there stone-faced, my date — a frail boy with a pudgy face — told me he could do nothing about the situation. I said, "Don't expect me to like this," a comment which would later earn me the title of "bitch" among his friends. I never sat with the fraternity section again; of course, I was never asked to.

My closest college friend was a closeted gay man with high political ambitions. This predicament, and his genius for comportment, made him quick to perceive and navigate the labyrinthine social rules of a status-conscious campus. Once, he introduced me to a student political leader in the African-American Association who wore wire-rimmed eyeglasses and a crisp, white oxford. Our conversation veered toward France and a shared interest in foreign film and beyond my friend's earshot he asked if I'd like to catch a movie.

"Sure," I said.

Later I mentioned this, and my friend replied, "He likes to date white women."

He had to say nothing more. I understood the implication. It was the source of fear in Mr. Smith's voice as he asked if I would attend the pubic schools, the reason we sat in isolated tables in the high-school cafeteria, the rationale for my mother's unwritten rules, the unspoken connection between these shard-like memories. What cuts the most — the silent compliance this world demanded and I gave.

Salt cuts the sugar, my mother had explained.

Attempts to Bury
History Backfire:
When Do the People Learn?

by KYES STEVENS

Race doesn't fit neat in me. It can't. I live in a small town in Alabama — a state where race is so loaded, you can rile up its barbed spirits in a tiny breath. Sometimes even the thought is enough.

It can't be neat, because when the fine white elders of the community where I reside talk to outsiders, they always mention the two active churches downtown. They don't include Mt. Travelers. I suppose it is because the congregation is black.

Even in Christian religion, a force that teaches its fold to follow the actions of Jesus, the bastions of the community here set up exclusion. They define difference. Without a developed consciousness that they are doing it I am sure, they reinforce an established and long-accepted hierarchical notion of societal existence. The lines of demarcation are still so solid here.

Race and the history of it in the South can't be neat because the town wants to control the number of black people moving in to its city-limits because most of the nice up-standing white folk don't want black people as their neighbors.

Race does not fit in neat with me because of my role in all this, by the history of it that I cannot change, and the unwillingness of people around me to accept their own part in this dynamic.

Everyday I am confronted with the capacity of cruelty and meanness based on generations of white folks and black folks being stupid with each other, holding grudges based on the actions of people who've been dead for years.

How can someone from Alabama think about race without thinking

145

of history, which opens up a never-ending pit in the soul, in the universe, another great wrong to blister our understanding of the past.

But...

This particular story does not start today, in this town. It starts in 1980 when my family moved to Jasper, Alabama — the town at the time had the reputation of being the place in the whole U.S. where you could hire someone for the least amount of money to kill another. I have recollections of bodies being found in refrigerators at the edge of lots — and blips from the evening news still sound in my memory. There was the ever-present air of caution that lingered in us through a childhood of wandering in the woods, exploring, and building forts. Danger was a presence. (It is unfortunate that my developed awareness of the capacity of human beings to be so cruel is aligned with my years in Jasper. The first realization always cements lasting impact — the mind holds on to the place.)

Up until the time we moved there, the only ongoing interaction I had with a black person was with Annie Mae — my paternal grandmother's house-keeper. To this day, I feel her take me up, and squeeze me good and call me sugar-baby. Those words illicit comfort like the love of my mother. All my grandparents have been dead for years. Annie Mae is still alive — the same age as my kin would be — hers the hardest life, still breathing. These is significance in this — just as the embarrassment that my rich and manipulative grandmother has a black maid. Annie Mae worked and my grandmother stayed in bed, reading and watching TV.

When we moved to Jasper some well-meaning white woman in the neighborhood told my mother upon hearing that we were Catholic that being Catholic around there was worse than being a n*****. Our neighborhood, we later found out from the nice, compassionate privileged white folk in town, was the wrong side of town.

My mother told me later that she wanted to move immediately. But we couldn't. That is where the work was. Work equals money and that sets up different rules for the game, for what a heart endures because that is where the job is, which is how you support your family. That is one justification process. Another is that no matter the cost, a person should not compromise his or her moral beliefs (but I think we are a nation of people that bend our moral beliefs to fit our own needs. I know of no one who does not get sucked in to the system of working for the dollar, and put up with and ignore all kinds of crap.) So, these early years of my life I lived in a place that discriminated against all kinds of minorities. But I assure you, Jasper does not hold this title singularly — it is shared by every place in this state that holds a handful or more of people.

I don't ever remember us as a family talking about race and discrimination when I was young. It was not brought to my attention by an adult, that I remember. These were the years of razors in Halloween apples, Tylenol gone bad, and all kinds of precautions and hazards to now be aware of—we had bad seeds tampering with things that would affect large numbers of people. Did race get lost in this? Was there concern just as much for the white child and black child who got contaminated candy? It is not so different from today when the Amber Alert goes out for white and wealthy children, and our media cannot get enough — like this abduction is the most important thing on the new — but when it is black children, it is a slight interruption of news on the screen.

We lived in West Jasper. After school, my brother Frank and I stayed with a sitter at our own home, a woman named Tobe who would help with housekeeping. My mother worked very long hours with her home-health care job. Sometimes we'd go pick Tobe up on the way home after school when her car was not working. We'd drive to the projects a spit down the road from our house — because that's what they were called — projects — that is what we called them (now the language is so loaded — reminds me of the syphilis study at Tuskegee). But because those were the words used around me that is what I learned. I do remember sitting in the hot car, riding around looking at everyone living in the apartments. I think I was jealous of folks living in apartments because what I saw were children everywhere, right next to each other, not like our neighborhood where the children seemed so far away. I think now I was drawn to the idea of community — something I did not understand at that time, but something I think I longed for. I also remember that when we got to Tobe's apartment, I had to get out of the front seat and move to the back. Adults rode in the front. One day we arrived at our house early to find Tobe loading laundry into the back of her car. From my recollection, my mother was not infinitely pleased with this. My mother's response intimated to Tobe that she really didn't care if Tobe washed clothes, but her hiding it was problematic. Some big lie. Something to hide.

We were taught not to do something without the permission of another, but what this leaves out is circumstance and opportunity. I don't know what Tobe thought of us. Maybe what she saw was white folks with money — *it wouldn't hurt us if she washed some clothes*. I was a child, but what she saw, I imagine, was a way to fill a need. I know that if she had asked my mother, Mom would have said yes.

But how would Tobe know this. I suppose what she knew was history. And poverty. And that we had a washer and dryer at the house.

How could she know that when we lived in Columbiana, just like everyone else who did not have enough money for a washer and dryer, we went to the laundromat next to a store that sold Cokes and candy that children stuck at the laundry against their will drooled over and scoured the streets and ditches looking for bottles to turn in for change. The laundromat had those slick plastic banana scoop chairs — and we would sit there waiting the cycles out — wash and dry, wash and dry. Fold. I always remember wanting to put coins in the laundry-supply machine and get Tide — because that is what I saw on TV, but that cost more than the others. I wanted to use dryer sheets — but growing up, that was an unnecessary expense. Maybe Tobe did not know that we knew what it was like not having a washer and dryer at home and Mom saving quarters so we could get them. I remember that jar and the coins placed there. This became a foundation for me. If I just worked hard enough and saved money, I could attain anything. The crock of crap that is the American Dream that people continue to believe is actually possible for everyone. Mom worked and she saved. But Mom got to go to college in the 1960s — got a scholarship, and went. This is not the reality of everyone. Nope.

Did my presence at the laundry event plant in me a moral high ground, the simple right-or-wrong reply, rather than the compassionate one? Was I being taught to see either/or — black or white, no shades of grey — rather than being taught to examine the *why* of what someone was doing something and figuring out a way to fix that?

For our first year-and-a-half of school my brother Frank and I went to West Jasper Elementary School. Mom took us to school most — in the diesel Impala, we'd move through the working class neighborhood singing, "Oh what a beautiful morning, oh what a beautiful day.... I've got a beautiful feeling, that everything's going my way." There we were going to school with all the poor folks — both white and black — who lived on the wrong side of town with us (of course, how could I know at that time that discrimination is also based on class — not just the color of your skin. It would take me many years to comprehend this, and then to identify those tendencies in myself). Robby, who lived in a trailer, and Shane, who also lived in a trailer, were the kids we played with, rode bikes with, had mud fights with. Somewhere I was taught that trailers meant poor — and that poor somehow meant that character was lacking in the people who lived in those trailers. So, even though they were my friends, they lived in *trailers*. Shane whose dad took the time to show me how to fix stuff on my bike, who worked on the railroad and got hit by a train, and Gravell who lived across Highway 78 at the junkyard. I remember playing hide and seek in that junkyard one summer night as a highlight of childhood. It was dangerous I am sure, but pure fun — ducking and diving into rusty, beat up rides. I remember lying on the floor at school during nap time wondering where I was, and I remember going to Brownies, playing basketball, and reading *Mysterious Wysteria*.

But we left that school because Frank's fourth grade teacher told my parents he was mentally challenged because his handwriting and spelling were horrible. They wanted to put him in special classes. This did not fly with the folks. Why should it? Frank could take Legos and build a crane that scooped up other pieces of the floor. No directions needed or even available. He just did it.

But here is part of the problem. Frank, my lovely brother, who still does not spell well (and we have all learned to read his handwriting), he is an engineer who builds structures underground. So had my parents listened to that teacher, everything would be different. But they did not, and they made the commitment to drive us to another school. My parents made that an option, the time and money to drive us to school (even though it was not that far away). Most of the other children at West Jasper — that was not an option for them. Was it because we were a family who believed in education, and so many who are impoverished do not have a strong educational experience, and so how would they know there are other options? But those options usually require money. So all, white and black, were stuck.

Our parents moved us to Park Memorial Elementary School — not far from the house of Tallulah Bankhead — so you can imagine the nature of the neighborhood. Huge shaded and manicured yards. At Park the education was good, I guess — except for Mrs. Tipman, my fifth grade teacher, who did not like Catholics. There were conversations at the church that I was not supposed to hear that confirmed my suspicion that she did not like me much, given the amount of time I sat facing the back wall during class.

Back to Frank. He is a super-smart guy. Really. And if a school system — or teacher — could decide that my brother was slow, based on something as incidental as handwriting, then the arbitrary could define the fates of many. One person with a chip the size of Birmingham on his shoulder could screw up the life of a kid — a person.

It happened to children based on race and gender. It happened based on cleanliness and which students never had the money for school supplies or field trips. All these things to diminish, to beat down, and conceal.

At Park School I was in Campfire Girls — all white, of course, and just down the hill was the Park and Rec where I played all kinds of ball. I was a mostly happy and remarkably unaware kid then. I mean, I knew I was different from the other kids and constantly fought to become a part of something indefinable — the popular clicks — the children who had white-bread sandwiches, Doritos and Capri-Suns for lunch — children in Izod shirts and girls with those green and blue purses with the whales. But I was not aware that that the white world that I lived in was set up for me, that choices were made to keep me away from otherness, based on the quality of services offered to middle-class white folks being better than those offered to the poor and black.

There were no black children at Park Memorial. Certainly there were no black educators mentoring that sea of white. I was not really aware of this until I went to middle school — the only middle school for the city — where all of us were thrown in the same pimply pot of pre-teen craziness. And even then, what all this meant did not hit home. I knew there was difference and privilege, I am not sure that I understood the why (I don't think I really started to fully understand the why until I went to graduate school at Sarah Lawrence College in New York — until I got out of the South).

These thoughts and this awareness left me for many years. We moved again. I got busy going to an all-white private school in Auburn, when my family moved back to their home stomping grounds. My parents would not allow us to go to the county schools, because the quality of education was so poor. But on some level, what that meant to me, was that only black kids and poor white kids went to these schools, and the quality of education there was poor because the students were. I am embarrassed to admit this now, when it is clear that the reason the educational quality was poor *was* because the kids were black and poor white, and thus not deserving of the same educational opportunities as other more affluent folks, who could afford to send their children to private school. But this distinction made me feel better about myself. More secure. I could look at people and say, well.... I went to Lee Scott (which interestingly now is something I am not terribly proud of).

Looking back, at my adolescent years, in environments that were exclusive — a remarkably white and predictable life, I always stuck out. One, because our family did not have *that* kind of money — to exist clearly in that exclusiveness, I was there for the education, but I am realizing that I also stuck out because I was aware of difference and discrimination. The world of have and have-not can be drawn as a color line. And this color line gives white people options — you are automatically given the benefit of the doubt, in most cases, doors are opened for you, or at least shown to you.

I revisited briefly these understandings when I was in undergraduate classes at Auburn — in English classes specifically — where I began to truly look outside the box I was raised in. My box was not as tiny as others' though. This is because my mother — who was a home-health care physical therapist — who traveled all over to help folks recover from a plethora of physical maladies. Because of her, I interacted with people who were not like us. It was a gift to me growing up. But there was a divide between what was supported at school and the rest of the world. The rest of the world was so rich and diverse — filled with people not like us. School was drab, white. School was filled with lots of white children whose parents did not want them going to public school with black kids.

Even though we moved from Jasper in 1985, down to Waverly, that town and events there hold significant places for me. It was Jasper where I got to bend some gender expectations in the 6th grade. I was tall for my age, and not such as bad basketball player. Me and two of my other girl friends who I played sports with tried out for the boys' basketball team at the middle school because there was no girls' team. And we made it. Back then — pushing those boundaries. I always had physical strength to rely on. It came naturally, but now, I realized the greatest strength is compassion — and a whole lot of growing up in Alabama nourished that.

When I was in graduate school at Sarah Lawrence College in Bronxville, New York, I wrote a research paper on Lillian E. Smith and a concept called the ideology of the body. I sent proposals for this paper to several conferences and got accepted to one at Ole Miss. So on a Spring Break excursion, my girlfriend and I drove from New York south (in my truck, with my dog). We drove through Jasper and on a whim, after touring around the town for the first time in years, I decided to see if they would let me in Park Memorial School. I wanted to see how things had changed — to see if there were any skin colors different than mine sitting in those tiny desks. It took some convincing for the secretary to even ask the principal if I could walk around (our society being full of some seriously bad folks, I could understand the hesitancy). My hair was intensely short and I had a lot of earrings (I went through a busting-out stage in NY). But when I explained that I had been a student there — the principal asked some questions — come to find out, I was the same age as her son — she remembered me. So, she permitted me to walk around. I walked down the first hallway that I had a class on — to Ms. Gray's third grade class. The hall much the same, the artwork same kid flavors. Then down the hall toward the gym toward Ms. Dollar's 4th grade class, and then Ms. Tipman... those rooms on the way to the gym.

There was not a black person there. Not a one. In 1999.

I wanted to know if my former classmates thought about this. I still want to know ... want to track down the handful that I remember and see what they remember, what they think.

So, I think about this history. This past. The privilege afforded me because I am white and because my family is middle-class. I always wanted to fit in, but by the nature of my development and my family, in some ways I could not, but I fit in to mainstream more than many folks.

Thinking about racism and classism, it informs most everything I do — as a poet, as a photographer, as a Town Council member, this history haunts me.

There is a significant history of white folks trying to "save" black folks. I did a good bit of research on it, focusing on the Depression era: white folks always thinking that they can do it better, that they know more. But it does get to the question: do I do more for my poor neighbors because they are black? I don't think so. I think I do for them because they are my neighbors, and there are children there, and I believe that children should know the goodness of people.

What my poor black neighbors are teaching me now is that I have to confront some real internal demons and be realistic with myself, about how I acknowledge and confront the role of race in my life.

My neighbors have indeed stolen water from our town — repeatedly. And they did destroy equipment — repeatedly. But this does not warrant a self-proclaimed savior of the community to pour motor oil in their other water source, an event he continues to wear as a badge of his commitment to upholding the goodness of our town.

All these wrongs. All these people acting-a-fool.

If we cannot, here, in this small town, work toward preventing the problem from occurring in the first place, if we refuse to address larger societal issues that influence the actions of the people, then what hope do we have outside of here, in some other Southern place?

Violence and vindictiveness do not stop violence and vindictiveness.

If I had fallen on hard times and could not pay my bill, and even if I stole water, I find it hard to believe that someone would pour oil in my water, here, in this town so many see as the idyllic place to be.

This setting up and treating differently is a problem — especially when it is so hinged on race, which is buried in the history here — and things buried in the rich Southern soil, the rain either exposes them again or nourishes the roots.

I am on the Town Council where I live. This little spec of a place. We have an unspoken, generations-long code of inequality — separation and judgment. But I don't fit in that either — our family never has (and that I would say is due to the fact that we did not go to church in this small town ... that the Methodist and Baptist churches were how the community was defined, and since we did not participate, we were on the outside).

Just maybe the difference is that I refuse to ignore injustice — it doesn't really matter if it is based on skin color, economic status, gender, or sexuality. Really, what does all that matter anyway?

Race and otherness sit on my chest — they are anvils, stones — because I cannot leave my house without seeing injustice, the complicatedness of living. My neighbors up the road are economically impoverished, and for many, many years, the adults in the house have done plenty of things to get the town pissed off with them. Most of these issues revolve around water bills not paid, and city property destroyed, stealing and lies. It also has to do with the activities that take place in the house that most folks would not see as the best environment for children to be in.

But the faulty logic here is: wow, this person is stealing water, so what can we do to help them? Instead of: what a bad person you are! If our community decided on goodness, rather than contempt, how might things have gone differently?

I am surrounded by good people who daily break laws — let's be realistic about this, people who drink and drive, people who smoke dope, people who speed, people who bend the rules all the time, and they line up to cast stones at the poor black family that steals water.

People must be willing to look at themselves — where they fit. Examine the glass-house of your own life.

The choices of the parents dictate so much for the children. When I first started taking fish we'd caught over to the neighbors, the mother made her children come out on the front porch and look me. She told them that if I came to the door, that they could open it. *She is good white people.*

Good and white. This must have seemed such a contradiction to those kids at that time. But because the mother felt like she had to say that, then there certainly was a history. And there is. Many of the families around here — the white families — have tried to get the family out of the place where they have squatted for years — for as long as I have known them.

This is the thing: everybody craps on those kids. They are black and they are poor.

What chance do they have? Who stands up in their corner, to help them fight back against all the oppression that faces them. It is history, it is family, it is community, it is all these things.

In isolation and educational deprivation, how does one learn to break down race, here in this state? How do we move beyond the tragic and ongoing history of discrimination?

The Civil Rights Movement started change, but in our society we are lazy and content to complain about the wrongs in our respective communities, rather than dong something to fix the ills. We don't feel any pressure on a massive populous level, because there is nothing forcing a reaction. We do not have children dying in church bombings in Birmingham. We do not have lynchings. The physical violence that was is no longer a factor, so people believe we have civil rights. We're not taught in school that there continues to be a great divide between those that have and those that don't — and that in Alabama, if you go to a rural, and/or a predominantly black school, the quality of education you receive is a fraction of the rich white schools of Auburn and Mountain Brook.

My generation — we are too comfortable, too blind, too content to say it is not our problem. My generation worries about who is who at church, and what shoes they are going to buy, or what kind of gun they are getting. Most of the people my age, here, in this now, don't really care.

Hiding Next Door

by VALLIE LYNN WATSON

I started seventh grade at the premier private school in Montgomery, Alabama, a jolt from the public school in Houston, Texas, where I'd finished sixth grade. My parents, after thirty years away from the town in which they had grown up, decided to retire back to Montgomery. They had left around age twenty, neither raised with any money nor in the upper echelons of Montgomery society. My father had a career in television production that parlayed into increasingly higher management positions in the Middle East, eventually making a lot of money (by Montgomery standards) and becoming, with my mother, one of the most prominent young American couples in Riyadh, Saudi Arabia, in the 1970s and '80s, before moving to Houston in 1983.

The return to Montgomery began by hunting for the perfect home. I realize now how important this house was to their arrival. They wanted to come back to the hometown where they had never felt like they quite fit in, announcing in a big way: "We're here." They eventually chose a well-known Tudor, 3500 square feet on a couple of acres, perched above the corner of the two main streets in the historic district.

Montgomery is a town of about 200,000 people, the capital of Alabama, set in the center of the state. It's perhaps most well known for its role in the Civil Rights Movement. Many white people in Montgomery dealt with the integration of schools by moving their children to private school.

On the first day of seventh grade, I knew I was in the wrong place when everyone around me rose and stood as the teacher entered the classroom. I soon learned that most of the forty or so students in the seventh grade had been going to school together since kindergarten. These kids said "ma'am" and "sir," knew how to be refined at age twelve and thirteen. I felt invisible and hideously deformed at the same time, a freak.

155

I turned thirteen that November, and my parents — who wanted me to fit in as much as they wanted to, and to have the Montgomery opportunities they thought they'd missed when they were growing up — arranged through my dad's sister, a member of the country club, to have my birthday party there. Invitations went out, and a few days later my mother got a phone call from another mother. We'd forgotten to consider that the three black kids in my class would not be allowed to attend the party, as black guests were not welcome at the country club. We quickly made up an excuse about my party being too close to exams, and rescheduled it at our house, complete with a DJ and all.

Though the entire class came to my party, I wasn't comfortable at the school, and by the end of the year, was begging my parents to let me move to another school. It wasn't that anyone at school was mean or spiteful to me; in fact I remember many kindnesses and efforts to include me. I wanted to go to public school, but I knew that wouldn't happen, so I argued for a different private school, one that was known to be less stuffy.

My father's extended family, in his thirty-year absence, had married well and had themselves become major players in Montgomery society, deeply involved in this first private school. He, the more easy-going of my parents, wouldn't discuss my changing schools. At the time I thought he didn't want to face his family. I was quickly learning what a small town Montgomery was. It seemed like everyone knew I was so-and-so's niece, so-and-so's second cousin by marriage. I felt like I was being watched all the time.

I know now that my father desperately wanted for me what he didn't grow up with, to be from the right family, go to the right school, the right church, even if he was finding that, as an adult, he didn't care so much about those things. Certainly he'd found a different and satisfying sort of success in life, but being back in Montgomery made all those ostracized feelings — the feelings that many teenagers have in some form or fashion — seem to matter more than they should, especially when it came to his child.

After another year of fighting, I finally succeeded and started at the new private school in the ninth grade. I immediately felt comfortable, quickly making a best friend, Lisa. I didn't realize it, but some of the Montgomery mentality had sunk in. I felt like I was a step above my new class on the social scale. My family had become members of the country club by this time, and there was a big club dance that spring. All ninth graders in Montgomery whose parents were club members were allowed to invite four or five other people and their dates to the dance. While many ninth graders from my previous school had parents who were members, only I and one other guy from my current school did.

My mom and I selected who I'd invite: a few people from older, established families, a few from my church. I left out some of the people I'd become closest to. I talked to the other guy about the situation, trying to impress upon him how important it was that he follow my lead in who he invited. He agreed, or so I thought, but I was shocked when I saw his invitation list. I felt like he'd picked who he'd picked to spite me: scholarship kids, girls who slept around and wore tight black dresses instead of the requisite Laura Ashley.

By the eleventh grade I was compromising these standards, in the name of love. I was dating a bad boy, a college freshman who'd gone to public school. I was working at the mall and had found a whole new society of friends, including a girl named Helen who seemed enamored by my family's social position in Montgomery, our house, and my school.

The junior prom was held at the country club, and my bad-boy boyfriend had provided alcohol for me and all my friends. Somehow the police got called, parents got called, and the group of us and our parents ended back at my house. The bad boy took responsibility for the alcohol, but after Lisa and her parents left, I told my parents that bad boy was covering for Lisa, that she'd gotten the alcohol. This got back to Lisa, and soon we weren't friends anymore

My dad wasn't there that night, he'd returned to Saudi Arabia for some temporary work that was to last much longer than expected. My mom and I didn't join him; she wanted me to be able to finish school in the States. She didn't join him afterwards, either, even though I sensed that she had grown tired of the social complications of Montgomery. She seemed to have stopped playing the game, no longer volunteering at the museum, not going to church. She didn't have many friends. Her best friend was her cousin, Judy, who happily lived out in the country, and had no interest in the Montgomery social scene.

By the time I traveled to Mississippi, the next state over, for college, I was starting to become aware that maybe my parents didn't actually believe in the social business, that since we'd moved to Montgomery they had been struggling to be different than the fifty-year-olds they'd grown up to be. Montgomery had activated in them the old insecurities they had as teenagers, similar to the insecurities I'd felt when moving to Montgomery. I knew my parents to be kind, accepting people and I didn't like that their return to Montgomery affected those values.

The next few years weren't good ones for my mom, though with me in college and my dad in Saudi, no one noticed much. She was clinically depressed and rarely left that big, old house. During my junior year of college she was diagnosed with cancer. The hardest part of losing her will always be that the last few years of her life were so poor, especially compared to the glamorous decades before they returned to Montgomery. I took a semester off of college to stay with her in Montgomery. I started dating an old high school boyfriend while I was home, and knowing that I was about to lose the stability of family, the stability of home, it seemed that he came along at that time because I was supposed to marry him.

One of the few things that felt okay, right, at the time was that two weeks before she died, I was able to tell her that I was unofficially engaged, though we didn't tell anyone else for months. I thought that was the best gift I could give her, a feeling that I'd found happiness, had found someone to take care of me.

Two years later, my wedding reception was at the country club. I was twenty-three. Without my immediate family around, I was increasingly feeling that Montgomery had nothing left for me. I didn't want to fight to fit in anymore. I insisted we move to Mississippi a few months after our wedding, and more often than not, didn't go with my husband when he returned to Alabama to visit his family. After we split up a few years later, I was determined never to return to Montgomery again.

It had become an evil place to me, the place that had made my mother's final years miserable, a place that had made me, during my adolescence, sometimes feel like an unforgivable snob. I was embarrassed that I'd failed at marriage, didn't want to return to a place where I constantly felt judged. I stayed away for seven years. The only difficult part of not returning was that I couldn't visit my mother's grave. Then Judy died, something I'd never considered happening, and out of respect for my mom, I had to go to the funeral.

My father and sister came too, and my dad's sister had a small gathering of relatives and a few of my parents' oldest friends. I invited the only friend I still had in Montgomery, Helen. Helen was a drama queen. Her identity seemed to come from the attention she could garner from men, and she was the first to admit any relationship she got into was going to be wrought with disaster. She hadn't grown out of the Montgomery mentality and had become a social climber, only dating attorneys and such, friendly only with those who might advance her status and career. At the party, she expertly flirted with all the men, but particularly my younger cousin.

The trip to Montgomery was mostly a good one. I was so far removed from that life that I didn't feel haunted, as I'd feared. It was instead, cathartic: I was able to visit my mom's grave with family, then again by myself right before I left, see the extended family I'd forgotten I cared about, drive past my old house and school, and even the country club, without too much grief.

A week or so after I got back, I got an email from Helen that she was going on a date with my cousin. I was pissed. I thought it was a generally unspoken rule that one doesn't date a friend's relative or old boyfriend without making sure it was okay, and moreover, I knew the chaos that could come out of it, the explaining I might have to do. Helen created scenes wherever she went. But it scared me to feel like this, like those old insecurities about what Montgomery at large might think about me mattered again. I didn't want to care that whatever drama Helen might create would reflect on me.

It took a few months to realize what bothered me the most. I knew Helen had initially become my friend because she was attracted to what she considered upper crust. That was fine at seventeen, but it hurt to realize she still valued class over friendship. I had to question if she met me today, outside of Montgomery, if she'd chose to become my friend, and I concluded that she would not. Because outside of Montgomery, I don't exist in any particular social hierarchy. I've moved around a lot, and the people I meet don't care where I went to high school or what ball I debuted at. This situation with Helen had made those old identity issues resurface.

Over my thirty-four years I've lived in eight cities. I'm independent, and since my mom died, I haven't had a place to call home. When people ask where I'm from, sometimes I evade the question, because — though I was raised in several other places before moving to Montgomery at age twelve — the real answer is that I'm from Montgomery.

Aside from my first birthday party in Montgomery, I rarely dealt with racial issues. It seems to me that the Civil Rights Movement did not have its desired effect, at least in Montgomery. Like my parents, Montgomery continued to struggle with its concept of social appropriateness. Neither school I attended had many blacks. There wasn't one in my graduating class of thirty-seven. Besides those who served us at the country club, I rarely encountered a black person socially, didn't work with any at the mall. Though African Americans made up half of the population of Montgomery, their world was alien to me and my friends and my family. This was to our detriment. If we'd been in a society where we could intermingle naturally we'd be facing the reality that we're all just people, and perhaps we wouldn't be caught up in this intense battle of class.

Maybe I'm kidding myself. I suppose these battles go on in any insular environment. They probably go on all around me in my current academic environment, but somewhere along the way I stopped caring. Maybe that's why I'm angry at Helen, because she made me care about that stuff again. She made me feel judged on an identity that I thought I had shed, one I am scared of because I feel like that makes me an ugly person. Of feeling scared that I'm just a state line away from being sucked back in.

Elevator Music

by RAVI HOWARD

Growing up in Montgomery, I lived within walking distance of the Ben Moore Hotel, the one-time centerpiece of the black neighborhood called Centennial Hill. My parents went to an event there one evening in the early 1960s. The elevator doors opened, and there stood Martin Luther King, Jr. The Reverend King had already left Montgomery for Atlanta and a leadership role on a larger scale. He had returned for an event, a meeting or speech perhaps, and there he was in a hotel elevator on the corner of Jackson and High streets. The simple hellos my parents exchanged were not enough to make a footnote in anyone's history but their own, but I imagine such encounters were frequent for black citizens of Montgomery. King on an elevator. Rosa Parks at the market. Ralph Abernathy at the gas station. Even as a child of the 1980s in Montgomery, I had a chance to share space with Civil Rights legends, if only removed by a decade or two. I used to get my haircut at the Malden Brothers Barbershop in one of the storefronts beneath the Ben Moore. During a visit, one of the barbers told me that Martin Luther King used to get his haircut there, which made sense because the Dexter Avenue Baptist Church parsonage was just up the street. He told me the story with a bit of pride and excitement because CNN had visited to tape a segment on the barbershop and its famous customer.

The barbershop beneath the hotel became for me a powerful reminder of the Civil Rights Movement. The idea of shared space with historical figures helped me to understand what had happened in Montgomery. It was great, as a child of the 1980s to look into the same mirror that Martin Luther King, Jr., might have after a shave. It was also remarkable to think that his hair clippings were swept from the same floor as those from the rest of us. Such moments made the Civil Rights leader, and the movement, seem textured, real, and human.

Local landmarks around Montgomery gave children like me a personal connection to not just the ideas of the movement, but the bricks and mortar of a specific time that has affected the world. I have visited the same State Capitol steps where Jefferson Davis, George Wallace, and Martin Luther King, Jr., spoke on their visions for America. It seems that King's words were the only ones that proved to be timeless.

While his ideas have remained intact over the years, his old neighborhood has not. The Ben Moore Hotel is emblematic of what has been lost in the years since desegregation. The hotel, long ago shuttered, is now just a place where black people used to visit. Where we used to gather, eat and fellowship. For my generation, it is a place where things once happened. Such a point of view makes the Civil Rights Movement or racial issues seem distant, to the point where people would rather tout color-blindness as a virtue than to acknowledge the rich and varied stories of race in America.

Montgomery has provided a close-up view of the kind of history that lives off the page, offering access to the people and places behind the stories. As those places fade, the sense of history within those walls becomes more distant. Without the concrete reminders of what the Civil Rights Movement was, that era is sometimes reduced to sound clips and slogans that carry less weight and texture. *I Have a Dream! Free at Last!*

It was easy for me to sit in that downstairs barber's chair and imagine who had been there before me, but that upstairs elevator was a mystery, as were the rooms and hallways. What discussions and plans made inside those walls influenced American history? The Ben Moore Hotel has stories that the Holiday Inn does not. Likewise, it has stories that the first White House of the Confederacy, a few streets removed, can never tell.

The Bus Boycott happened a few years before my parents moved to Montgomery and eventually crossed paths with Dr. King, but they inherited lessons of that event. Those lessons they shared with me. I recall a visit to a Japanese steakhouse in Mississippi when I was seven or eight years old. After waiting a long time for service in a nearly empty corner of the restaurant, a white family was seated nearby and immediately served. A chef came to their table and started to dazzle the children with knife skills. There was no subtlety in what had happened, so my parents decided to leave. I wanted to stay, there were spinning knives and flying food after all, but my parents insisted. When we were in the car, they explained some things that I call The Montgomery Discipline, about black people not spending money where our dollars are not respected.

I have tried to live by that example over the years. A security guard at an Eddie Bauer store forced a young black man to remove a shirt he purchased on a previous visit and told him to come back with the receipt. I had frequented the store prior to that, but not since. A Macy's security guard harassed me in their New York store, and I have not made a purchase in one of their locations since. In the mid–1990s, Texaco executives were caught on tape using racial slurs to reference black employees. In the years since, I've bought gas elsewhere. If the black people of Montgomery could walk to work for a year to gain respect, then I could certainly drive to another gas station or find another department store.

The Montgomery Bus Boycott opened doors that many blacks in their twenties and thirties routinely enter without a second thought. In the minds of some, perhaps a stigma arose around their familiar institutions. Were those who had denied service for generations were more equipped to meet the needs of black patrons? Perhaps the newness of the Best Western was more appealing than the character of the Ben Moore Hotel. When the old landmarks began to close, young blacks in Montgomery missed a chance to see a black economic community that thrived not because of segregation but in spite of it.

In recent years, my wife and I returned to Alabama, as have many childhood friends. The enterprising spirit of my generation holds promise. Many have started businesses from the ground up, while others have taken the helm of family businesses that have existed for generations. Additionally, Montgomery seems to have homeowners and businesses eager to rediscover and develop downtown. Among the properties slated for redevelopment is the Ben Moore Hotel. I hope that my wife and I could perhaps visit one day, eat at the restaurant, and at some point ride the elevator. The symbolic parallels abound. Uplift. Arrival. Ascension is part of the design. Doors that once opened for my parents to reveal a hero of their times, can continue to open for the rest of us, again and again.

What Is There to Say?

by RAY MORTON

When asked to write an essay about being raised by parents who had come of age during the Civil Rights Movement, I stared at the computer screen asking myself, "What should I write?" and "What do I have to say?" I am just an ordinary person who happened to be raised in a Deep South state — Alabama. I never had much contact with African Americans growing up, and I certainly did not have any kind of unique story to tell, no epic tale about the struggle for equality or even of witnessing significant Klan activity. Just normal, so I figured I would write about my childhood and as I began to ponder on what to say, I, in fact, did have a story to offer — one of personal change.

I was born in Greensboro, North Carolina, but moved to Birmingham prior to my first birthday. My mother, who was from Ohio, had never seen Black people until she was eighteen. She was raised Catholic, so her ideas of social justice were very strong regarding African Americans. My father was born and raised in Birmingham, Alabama, and came of age during the Civil Rights Movement. He would have been 13 in 1964, during Project X and the Sixteenth Street Baptist Church bombing. My grandparents worked downtown and had very clear ideas about race and the "place" of African Americans. They held, what we would historically call, very Southern ideas about race. My grandmother had Black maids who worked for her in the 1960s and from what I can remember of conversations regarding what seemed to be very devoted, friendly persons, none were ever seen as equals. These ideas were ingrained in my father and passed down to me at a young age. We were not Klan members but "nigger" was heard from time to time; there were not discussions that African Americans were beneath us, but it was just understood. We did not have Black friends and if we wanted to maintain our extended family we certainly did not date, or even joke about dating, Black women.

Throughout my high school career, race was never an issue. Things were just the way things were and it was not an issue. My mother never supported ideas of racial superiority of any sort and the word "nigger" was deemed a curse word even though my father and grandfather used it freely. She, however, was not the dominant of the two personalities in our household and her view often got overshadowed by my father's more dominant racist ideas. These ideas, though I never thought about them, seeped into my subconscious. I had a few Black friends, but they never came over to the house, and I never went to their houses and outside of school we never spoke — so, were we friends? I remember learning that an ancestor of mine had been the one who had been Nathan Bedford Forrest's Captain of Artillery, a good friend of the "Wizard of the Saddle," and also the one who had sworn Forrest into the Klan. I remember thinking that was so "cool" and being proud, not of the historical connection more or less, but of the fact that it was the Klan. I also remember in 1996 going to a Klan rally in downtown Birmingham and observing the pathetic gathering. I was not there to support it, mostly I was a casual observer, but I can also remember as I reflect back on not being appalled and disgusted.

Did I spend my time riding around in big trucks with Confederate flags looking for Blacks to harass? No, and if one had asked me during high school or college if I was a racist I would have said an emphatic "no," but as I moved through life and began studying Alabama and the Civil Rights Movement I began to learn that the activists in "Bombingham" were not "outside agitators" or people making it dangerous for "the good white folks to walk to work." They were simply a people who had been oppressed for centuries wanting only the most basic human rights.

As I began to learn more about what racism was in all forms and how it affected society I became more aware of my prejudices and my loose use of racial stereotypes and epithets. I also became aware that though I repeated a lot of the ideas that I had heard among my family and friends, I had always known that somehow those ideas were wrong and I was pretending to be someone that I really was not just to fit in with people. Maybe it was to fulfill a self-defeating image as a "true" Southerner. Anyway, I became more aware of this internal conflict and was faced with an identify crisis as I rejected the ideas of what I had been taught and about who I thought I was and merged a new set of ideas and a new image. It was not an overnight process or an easy one. I honestly have to say that in some ways I still struggle with it to this day.

As I learned more about tolerance, the Birmingham pledge, and the white role in racism, I began to further understand that while I was not blowing up churches or beating Freedom Riders my attitudes and views were racist and needed to change. I took my "pride" in my ancestral connection with the Klan and wrote a Master's thesis arguing scathingly about the dangers of the Klan, no matter how active they are or what time period it is, and their fascist ideas. I read more about slavery, the nadir of race relations at the turn of the 20th century, the Civil Rights Movement, and about discrimination today. I try my hardest to be tolerant and believe that, person to person, I give everyone an equal chance. I have tried to better myself and change my views, but ideas are hard to change sometimes and from time to time I catch myself thinking, sometimes aloud, stereotypical thoughts blanketing a group of people based on the rude actions of one individual who cuts me off in the middle of rush hour traffic.

Were parents who came of age during the Civil Rights Movement prepared to raise children in a post-segregation society? I think it depends on each family, but in my case no. Does that mean that everybody in my generation will be prepared to raise children with ideas of equality in mind? I think there will be a better chance that we will see a decline in these "Southern" ideas and certainly less of an excuse available for those with racist ideas. They will no longer be able to say, "Well, that is just the way it was," or that they did not know any better. Most, today, know that hate and inequality are wrong but it will always go back to the nurture effect and the idea that "hate not transformed, is hate transferred."

Facing South

by KATHLEEN ROONEY

Kathleen's father made eye contact in the rearview mirror of their wide blue pickup, the one with the topper over the wide blue flatbed that now contained many of their worldly possessions, and said, "We are not now, and we will never be Southerners."

He told her this when she was five, and her sisters were one and two, and he and her mother were moving them all from the city of Omaha in the county of Douglas in the state of Nebraska to the city of Shreveport in the Parish of Caddo in the state of Louisiana in 1985.

As Nebraska gave way to Kansas gave way to Missouri, he talked about history. About how Shreveport had been the capitol of Louisiana during the Civil War. And about how the Union General William Tecumseh Sherman had known, because of his military victories, that once the fighting was over, they would erect equestrian statues of him all over the North. He knew the sculptures would be out in the sun and the wind and the snow and the rain, and that squirrels would crawl over his boots, and little kids would rub his nose for luck, and pigeons would crap on his hat. But none of that bothered him as long as he could have the guarantee that whatever else they did to his big bronze likeness, they made sure to position his horse's ass facing due South.

Her dad would tell this story again three years later when Kathleen was eight and they were (finally, he said, finally) leaving Louisiana for Chicago, for the North, where they belonged.

Both times, Kathleen's mother leaned toward the back from the passenger seat, her dark hair in sharp contrast with the paleness of her face, and said in her flat Midwestern accent that this was a rude story and that Kathleen was not to repeat it. Kathleen agreed.

But Kathleen loved history and Kathleen loved to read and she read all she could about her family's new home. It had been founded in 1836 on land sold to the Shreve Town Company by the Caddo Indians in 1835. The blues singer Leadbelly had developed his style in the red light district. And Sam Cooke had been arrested there 1963 when he tried to check his band into a Holiday Inn for whites only.

In the Piney Woods of ArLaTexOma. Shreveport-Bossier City was supposed to be the cultural and commercial center, but it felt to Kathleen like the middle of nowhere, like the middle of some lost subtropical expedition — birds and bugs and plants she'd never seen — and this to her was lovely. Her mother disagreed.

Anole lizards crept in through the cracks in the foundation of their house, the slots between doors, and her mother kept shrieking when she found the creatures leaping along her counter tops and lurking in her cabinets. She had Kathleen chase them, catch them, and take them outside. Sometimes Kathleen would grab them, but they would wriggle and slip and she'd miss and they'd get away. Once, determined to capture a lizard that was particularly wily — she was only trying to help — she held on as its rough, dry green body — the body that could change, if camouflage were required, to brownish gray — slithered through her fingers, and she gripped the tail, thinking to hang on that way, when it came off and remained, light and twitching, in her hand as the lizard darted back under the floorboards and escaped. She cried and cried, showing the tail to her mother who told her to throw that thing in the yard, and she was not even comforted when her dad explained that this was natural, the lizards' escape mechanism, how they got away from birds and other predators when simply hiding didn't work.

It went on this way until Kathleen's father pointed out that the lizards ate the cockroaches, bigger than any they'd seen in the North, which found their way inside the house no matter how clean her mother kept it, and her mother let the creatures stay. One lizard lived in the Regulator clock that hung on the wall in the family room, ticking the seconds with its brass pendulum, ringing out each hour in jingle-bell time. The lizard stayed there for months, had babies, raised a family, and Kathleen never knew how they all fit, how they didn't get crushed by the wheels and gears.

Some things Kathleen liked about Shreveport. Some things she did not. She liked the Red River between Shreveport and Bossier and how the mud that gave it its color also gave it its name. She liked learning in school how the city was formerly a hub of steamboat traffic, of cotton and crops. They did not learn in class, but she read on her own, that it had also been a center for the trading of slaves.

She did not like how, one day, in the summer, when her mother had taken Kathleen and her sisters to the Red River Revel, a carnival on the waterfront, a blue-eyed woman had come up and looked at her sister Megan in the stroller, sized up her tan skin and kinky hair, and said to her mother that she looked like a black man's baby. This was not meant to be understood as any kind of good thing. Kathleen did not like how her mother had just stood still, not knowing what to say, until the woman walked away. "Why didn't you tell her that Dad is white?" Kathleen asked her mother, who stood there looking dumbstruck. "Because that woman was impolite," her mother said, "and because if you can't think of anything nice to say, it is better not to say anything at all."

Kathleen liked the way the people in Shreveport talked, but her parents did not, or at least they did not want their daughter to talk in that way. If she came home and said *y'all*, if she came home and asked somebody to *pull the door to*, if she came home and announced she was *fixin' to do* her homework, then, "What did you say?" her mother would ask. "Say that again," her father would command. And she would repeat the offending phrase, and the telltale trace of Southern speech would be excised, redacted, revised, replaced with the proper way of talking: *all of you. Please shut the door. I'm about to do my homework.*

She liked the huge yard — almost an acre — behind their small ranch house with the honeysuckle, the fig tree, the crabapple, the wild strawberries, and the fence that divided their garden from that of Mr. Whitley, who used to give them collard greens.

Most of all, she liked the dozens of live oaks, their gnarled branches running through the dangling Spanish moss like bony fingers combing ghostly hair. In the early spring it seemed as though the trees conspired to drop all their leaves at once. Her dad worked long hours during the week and did Air Force Reserves on the weekends, and her mother wasn't about to tackle the job all by herself, so they looked in the phonebook and hired a team of men from a yardwork company to come rake the leaves for them. The team turned out to be just a regular family, and all of them — the mom, the dad, and four kids ranging from Kathleen's age on up to what must have been 15 or 16 — worked all morning putting the leaves in piles that were almost big enough to remind her of Nebraska haystacks. When they'd finished making the heaps and were about to put them in sacks to be hauled away — maybe mulched, probably burnt — Kathleen's mother stuck her head out the screen door — it was already warm enough to have the windows open — and said, "You must be hungry. I've made some baloney sandwiches, and some peanut butter ones. I've got some lemonade too, if you'd like to come in and have a bite to eat."

The kids all looked at Kathleen's mom like she had gone insane, and their mother started raking again at some imaginary leaves. The dad shrugged his shoulders and said, "Thank you very much, ma'am. That would be awfully nice. But we really can't come in."

"What do you mean?" Kathleen's mother replied. "You've been working hard all morning. I don't mind if you take a break."

"It's not you that I think would mind, ma'am," the man said. "I just don't think some of your neighbors would like it if they saw people like you let people like us come inside your house."

What the man meant, Kathleen knew, was that he, his wife, and all their kids were black, and that Kathleen's mom, her husband, and all her kids were white. Kathleen's mother compromised and brought the food out. The family took off their gloves, set their rakes aside, and ate and drank quickly on the patio before finishing up the job and driving away.

Kathleen liked the kid named Terrell in her second grade class who sat right behind her in the rows of desks because of their last names: she was an R, and he was an S. She liked Terrell, but she got the sense that she was maybe not supposed to. Most of the other kids in her class she knew already, not just from kindergarten and first grade, but from her neighborhood. And while the school — like the city — was a little less than half black, none of the black students lived on her street, near her family or her other friends' families. And for the most part, none of them ended up in her class, but instead were next door, in the class down the hall. "Why are you hanging out with him?" and "I don't know why you want to play with that weird kid," and worse they said at lunch, in gym class, on the playground to Kathleen if she sat by Terrell , threw the ball to him, or tagged him the Goose in Duck Duck Goose. When her mother called the school to ask how it could be possible that all the kids of one type ended up in one class while all the other kids ended up in another, the principal, Miss Booty, whose name was a source of much hilarity, said that it had been a coincidence, and besides, it wasn't entirely like that — after all, just look at Terrell.

Her mother might have made a bigger deal had they stuck around longer, but that spring her dad got a better job, their small ranch house sold, and they packed up the pickup and moved up to Illinois. Kathleen finished the last few weeks of second grade in a school outside Chicago. Her Shreveport best friend Lisa, also from the North, from Buffalo, New York, had promised Kathleen she would pick up her yearbook, and would get it signed by all her friends. When it arrived in the mail and she opened it up, Kathleen was pleased, even pleasantly surprised, to see that Lisa had gone out of her way to include Terrell , who had signed the page near his black and white photograph in green ink, in poor penmanship, "The Weird Kid." She put the book away. It and Louisiana became two of many things about which she never really thought.

Until later.

Kathleen was 27 going on 28, back in Illinois after being away a long time to both coasts East and West. She was now working in the office of Illinois' senior senator, and her position put her in close proximity to the hopeful campaign of an African-American man, the junior senator from her state, who was running for president. Her job also put her in proximity with lots of co-workers of different races, and this was one of the many aspects of this job that she liked.

And when she sat in meetings with these people, her friends, and they joked around or went down sidetracks that had to do with stereotypes about class or race, she thought to herself about how her parents were not pioneers, nor even especially progressive in their own attitudes.

She thought about this when her co-worker Steve, a white guy about her age, came in one Monday and told the story of how he'd been mugged over the weekend. Coming home from a party, he'd been about two blocks from his apartment when he saw two thuggish teenagers walking his direction beneath the cone of a streetlight. "I got a bad vibe from them," he said, "and I thought about crossing the street, but they were two young black guys and I didn't want to be rude. I didn't want to be the guy who crossed the street just because he saw a couple people of a different race. They took out a gun, stole my wallet and everything in it, plus my cellphone, and made me lay on the ground and count to thirty while they ran away. Later, when the cops asked me if I wanted to file a report and press charges, I said 'I don't know,' because I really didn't know — I hadn't thought that far ahead. They asked me who I worked for, and they said I was too liberal and that people like me are what's wrong with this country."

Like Steve, Kathleen's parents were simply Midwestern and polite, and they believed that manners were the first best defense against total social decay and barbaric chaos, and that it would be rude not to socialize with another child because he happened to be black, and that it would be rude not to offer someone food for the same reason, just as it would have been rude for Steve to have crossed the street that night. But they never really dealt with it. They never really figured it out, or fixed it, or had to face it head-on.

And sometimes such attempts at politeness were goofy. Kathleen thought about this as she and her co-workers pulled numbers for the driving pool — deciding who would drive the Senator around the city and when — and her co-worker Nia, a black woman, told them how funny it was that whenever it was her turn behind the wheel, "The Big Guy turns the radio to black people music: Motown, hip-hop, you name it. I'm tempted to tell him that despite appearances, I don't listen to that stuff all the time."

And sometimes people were goofy and impolite. At one staff meeting, Kathleen and her co-worker Lamont, a black man, told about how they'd been working the phones together, and a persistent constituent, an elderly black lady from the city's West Side, had called once and asked a question and gotten an answer from Lamont, and then called again and asked a much harder question — one requiring research and a returned call at a later time — of Kathleen. The lady had gotten so angry that she said she would call all the radio and TV stations and tell them that Kathleen refused to help her unless Kathleen got off the line and gave the phone back to "that nice young black gentleman who helped me the other time."

Kathleen and her co-worker Andrew, a blonde guy from Wisconsin, drove south to see the African-American candidate speak on the campaign trail at the end of 2007. But they were only headed as far as South Des Moines, and as they drove under the cold stars of the Iowa night, they talked about how this candidate's mixed race was one of the things that made him attractive to them — that made them, as was his main message, feel audacious and hopeful — although mostly the issue remained unspoken, undealt with, and when it did come up, it turned ugly quickly. When it did come up, critics would often suggest that the black candidate was not black *enough*, that he was more from Indonesia, more from Hawaii, than he was from any place to which most American black people could relate.

Shortly after that trip, Kathleen's number was up in the driving pool. As it happened, this was during a week when the black candidate's main opponent, the woman who wanted to be the first female president of the United States, had been accused of making remarks that could be construed as belittling the achievements of Dr. Martin Luther King, Jr., whom the black candidate quoted frequently. Kathleen's boss, the senior senator, thought that this debate was foolish and depressing, and should just be dropped, left behind, but on the pundits went on, debating it anyway.

Kathleen was not so sure it could be abandoned so decisively. The race card, her boss thought, had no business being played by either side. Kathleen had a hard time seeing how it couldn't be played. She was waiting with the engine idling in a heavy silver sedan outside a TV studio beside the Chicago River while her boss taped an interview on the subject. She thought of how the next big primary battle was to be in South Carolina, the first Southern state to vote, and she wondered to herself how it might turn out "down there." She thought of the anole lizards, and she thought of their tails, and of how leaving part of yourself behind completely was not an ideal way to escape, and that some things couldn't be completely excised and that they probably shouldn't be, that they shouldn't be tossed off and dismissed so easily.

She thought about mentioning this to her boss when he and the press secretary emerged, squinting in the winter sunlight, from the revolving door at the side of the building. But then she thought it might be rude to bother her boss that way, so she put on her sunglasses, buckled her seatbelt, waited for them to do the same. Then she made eye contact with her boss in the rearview mirror and started to drive.

Afterword

by David Molina

I'm not from around here. Not from the South generally, and not from Mississippi in particular. Born in inner city St. Louis, I spent my youth and adolescence in the suburbs on the west side of Cleveland, Ohio, and my college years in western Massachusetts. Initially, I came down to Mississippi as a participant in the Mississippi Teacher Corps — a two-year, alternate-route teaching program funded by the state and run through the University of Mississippi. As of this writing, I'm in the midst of my sixth year here: first as a public high school teacher in Jackson, then as a project coordinator at the William Winter Institute for Racial Reconciliation (situated in Oxford at Ole Miss but with work primarily focused on communities throughout the state), and now as staff member for the University's Center for Writing and Rhetoric.

"How did you end up here?" and, as the years accumulate, "Why did you stay?" are questions that have come up again and again as I've lived and worked in Mississippi, whether in Jackson teaching Algebra, in Greenwood facilitating intercommunity dialogue, or in The Grove for an Ole Miss game. Questions in this vein are perhaps my most common explicit experiences of negotiating the South as a non–Southerner — of the need to, quite literally it seems, ground one's voice in order to justify it. I've very rarely found this to be a hostile inquiry, though. While you're-not-from-around-here moments do carry historical, cultural and geographic weight, that may just as well be a consequence of the sheer historical and cultural weight of these geographies. Being here in Mississippi, for better or for worse, is often as much about "here" itself as it is about my (or anyone else's) being here. Take, for instance, the University of Mississippi, an institution I've been affiliated with in one way or another since I've been in the state. I've found that the very grounds hold histories — sometimes in conflict, always in conversation; histories that fold into themselves,

become their own commentaries, ironies, revisions. A five-minute walk
through the Ole Miss campus can bring you by the stained glass window
depicting the University Grays, the Confederate monument, the bullet
holes in the Lyceum, the statue of James Meredith. Like the rings of an
old tree — this year rain, this year fire, this year drought — except a tree
both bred and cut from the burden of time.

Though I possess a sincere and growing affinity for the communities
I've come to navigate and negotiate while being here, it is nevertheless
true that I did not grow up in the South, did not come of age in the South,
and — in regards to crucible of history, culture, region, and conflict — I
am not, and in many ways will never be, Southern. While this does not
determine my experience, it certainly informs it. As I see it, so much (perhaps all) about identity — not only regional identity but race, gender, sexuality, class, and so on — is absent without context, especially that initial,
power-laden context of difference: establishing and understanding some
as *us* and some as *them*. And, in my experience of the South, the regional
us/them difference still holds profound and at times central weight, especially in those moments when Southern identity is tied to racial identity
and racial conflict.

That being said, I have, at times, found it difficult to ground myself
in this place. Especially in that first year: wherein I found myself with 150
students (all black; there were and are only a handful of white students at
Jim Hill High School in Jackson), almost no textbooks, and only the most
naïve notions of how to help young people figure out how to solve linear
systems. And, let's be honest: in 2005 I was an ostensibly white guy from
a liberal New England college who'd grown up in the North and come
down to Mississippi to teach mathematics in an essentially all-black public
high school in Jackson. *Yankee, liberal, carpetbagger, outside agitator.* My
story was written for me, or so I felt whenever I addressed a "how'd you
end up here" query by students, coworkers, or friends. There was certainly
a sense that I would have to work myself out of a narrative (i.e. "the non–
Southerner") as much as I would have to work myself into one (i.e. "being
here"). However, as I've found myself more and more fluent in the rhythms
and spaces of these communities, I find the need to explain my non–South-
ernness to be rarer and rarer. Somehow I've approached the somewhat less
complicated position of both not being "from here," but also having "been
here" for a while. Or at least long enough not to feel like I have to explain
myself as much as I used to.

While working for the Winter Institute, I would often face an additional moment of incredulity after telling someone that I was working for

an "Institute for Racial Reconciliation." Nearly everyone felt compelled to ask, "So what exactly does your institute *do*?" More often that not, this would amplify the already pressing need to "ground my voice in order to justify it." Essentially, "you're-not-from-around-here" became "you're from *where* and you're *here* doing *what*?" My answer would satisfy almost no one: essentially, "It depends on the community. And, yes, I grew up in Ohio."

For, during my time there, the Winter Institute did not go into a community unless invited to do so, and when it did it deferred to local leadership and expertise in determining the most important legacies of racial identity and conflict in their community, and in deciding how to best engage those legacies. So there really wasn't a set list of services the Institute provided, nor was there a set way that it measured/defined progress in "racial reconciliation." It saw itself as a highly adaptive entity, seeking to equip communities to heal their own wounds and citizens to heal their own communities. One week we'd be in Tallahatchie County assisting citizens in issuing a public statement of regret in regards the Emmett Till murder and trial; another week we'd be in Jackson working with young people looking to establish a youth-generated media outlet at a local newspaper; another week we'd be helping facilitate a student-led retreat for Ole Miss students looking to address issues of social segregation on campus. Needless to say, it was an interesting job.

However, no matter where the Institute ended up with communities, it always started in the same place with them: the act of bringing a diverse and representative group together, and helping them to start talking *with* each other — not *about* each other. Whenever we went into a community, we always began with the same, simple approach to dialogue: we would sit people down in a circle, share some ground rules, and ask everyone to respond — from their own experience — to the following:

Tell a story about the first time you realized that race was the "elephant in the room"— something that everyone noticed but no one talked about, something that was big, and there, and affected everything despite our best efforts to ignore it.

This "story circle" was conducted without cross talk and commentary, which could only take place once all the stories were shared. Everyone was asked to tell a single story from their experience and asked to simply listen while others do the same. Where we'd go from that initial conversation depended on the individuals in the circle, the community represented, and the narratives uncovered. And while it was hardly the Institute's claim to understand what would be *sufficient* for improving race relations or achieving racial reconciliation in that particular community, there was, however, a firm claim of understanding what would be *necessary* for those things: that people can talk with each other, can listen to each other, and can allow each other's narratives into the circle.

In reading the essays in this book I was reminded again and again of the Winter Institute's use of the story circle as a starting point for the reconciliation process. The stories here are a powerful reminder of how personal narratives can be used as a framework for critically reflecting upon the legacy of race and racism in our lives and communities. Many moments in these pages could very well have been lifted from any one of the many, many story circles I've participated in or facilitated in communities throughout Mississippi. Of course, no one sat these writers down and gave them the "elephant in the room" prompt, but each story is nevertheless similarly haunted with those moments wherein time balloons and halts as the storyteller bears witness to an unmistakable union of race and power — moments at once roiling with confusion, searing with anger, and thick with guilt: Anne Gray Brown's "conversion" note; Jim Grimsley's "black bitch" exchange; Anne Estepp's utterance of "nigger"; Dawne Shand in a swimming pool; Ravi Howard in a restaurant; Glenis Redmond in a sundown-town. Present as well in these stories is the sense that so much about who we are or how we view the world is an aftermath to these "elephant" moments. What we see in these essays can hardly unearth a first encounter with the intense consequences of racial identity without discussing as well the long, essential process of coming to terms: Georgene Bess Montgomery and the legacy of her "two childhoods"; Stephanie Powell Watts looking back with pride/nostalgia at an early and "ephemeral" moment of racial inclusion; Vallie Lynn Waston feeling a deep sense of being out of place; Leslie Haynsworth confronting the "zero-sum game" of race, gender, motherhood, and opportunity; Ray Morton slowly unraveling and re-imagining white Southern identity.

Born in 1982, I'm two-to-three generations removed from the common Civil Rights era, and I've certainly spent plenty of my adult life trying to make sense of my identity in the context of race, class, and history. So, in many ways I can relate to the generational shift Foster Dickson outlines in his introduction to this book: there is the generation who experienced life under segregation and the end of so many laws and practices that characterized the institutional manifestation of white supremacy, the generation that grew up in the direct and immediate effects of that change, and now a generation or two (or three) living in the aftermath: pushed from behind by historical revision and pulled from the front by the post-racial promise.

That being said, what is perhaps most striking about this set of essays, most of which are set in childhoods that range from the 1960s to the 1980s, is their commonality. This was a similar experience in the many story circles I conducted as a member of the Winter Institute. Whether it was an eighty-year-old white judge, a middle-aged black businesswoman, or a mixed-race teen, structural similarities across stories illuminated a landscape of common experience. This allowed, as it does in this book, for a potentially unifying context — that these deeply personal narratives, while at times completely different, are not altogether disjoint. Whether *A* or *B*, I learned about race from my parents, my teachers, and other adults; whether *P* or *Q*, my sense of race was defined by that one moment, that one word; whether *X* or *Y*, I grew up with racial conflict lurking just around every corner. These and other structures provide potential bridges across the varied experiences of the legacy of race and racism — whether we are with Georgene Bess Montgomery remembering how the presence of truckloads of white men outside her house "murdered her sleep" or whether we are with Jaqueline Wheelock reflecting on the "baggage [of] infused fear [and] embedded inferiority"; whether we are with Jim Grimsley as his father points out "the nigger school" lest his children forget, or whether we are with Anne Estepp getting slapped on the mouth by her mother for reciting an epithet-tinged version of the children's rhyme "eeny, meeny, miney, moe, catch a tiger by the toe."

Especially given the challenges of historical memory presented to my and future generations — now further and further away from the major cultural and civic shifts of the Civil Rights era — I think it is the ahistorical nature of these narrative similarities that will allow us to continue to unravel the legacy of race and racism in ourselves and in our communities. Surely these stories are grounded in historical memory, and surely our lives are informed by generations of cultural tradition. But, the sheer separateness of the *us/them* divide can obscure the possibility for an easily shared language of history and culture. The act of having to communicate one's story across difference may begin to bridge this miscommunication. Whether eighteen or eighty-five, whether middle-class black or poor white, whether Southern or not, there is a kernel of truth in the mere legitimacy of someone's perspective, in the value of their memory. It is the listener's acknowledgement of this truth that the story circle values, that these essays illuminate. We all live in these legacies, we are all informed by these legacies, we all suffer from and/or thrive within these legacies; now let us speak from within them in a way that does justice to the sheer validity our experiences, and let us listen in a way that honors that validity. As we do justice to each other's narratives in this way, as we find common ground in similarities that sit beyond the complexities history, race, and culture that we must speak through, we work towards the rehumanization and disalienation of each other. Furthermore, it is exactly through this process of rehumanization and disalienation that we can then unravel those complexities of history, race, and culture that initially brought us to the circle. In other words, I may not acknowledge, let alone value, difference until I begin to value someone speaking from within difference, so we must start talking *with* each other — not *about* each other — before we can even begin to consider the possibility of reconciling these differences.

Of course, accepting the possibility of race as a dehumanizing and alienating force — even an existing force, in some cases — is necessary for this process of narrative justice to even begin. In "Why it Matters," after recounting a method for discovering a possible African-American ancestry in her father's family — which had previously been "explained away" as "Indian blood" — and encountering her father's constant refusal to have a DNA test to determine his heritage, Anne Estepp offers the following:

> That's when I realized that even in my hometown, where everyone is white, race matters. It's just that no one wants it to matter because that makes things too difficult; it opens a new can of worms.... Race is too abstract, too inconceivable, and at the end of the day, too disturbing.

Here, Ms. Estepp skillfully demonstrates that all-too-common notion that exploring the impact of race and racism upon our identities would risk unhinging a kind of Pandora's box — even in a town that assumes itself to be all white (which sets up inevitable and innumerable historical ironies). However, it is exactly this attitude of avoidance, in its preemptive fear of letting race "matter," that actually gives it more ways of mattering — that transforms it into the "wolf [we have] by the ears, and we can neither hold him, nor safely let him go." In fact, as we see in all the essays of this book, race is not wholly abstract, because we experience it; race is not wholly inconceivable, because we can articulate it; race is not wholly disturbing, because we can find comfort and support in it and life beyond it. What this book embodies is exactly the sort of honest engagement in both individual and collective memory that will take such an "abstract," "inconceivable," and "disturbing" a thing as race and illustrate how it informs the specificity of our lives, but does not determine them — thus showing it in the light of experience rather than the shadows of suspicion.

In *Black Skin, White Masks*, Franz Fanon declares: "The body of history does not determine a single one of my actions. I am my own foundation. And it is by going beyond the historical, instrumental hypothesis that I will initiate the cycle of my own freedom." For, while Foster Dickson is right in his introduction to consider the adage that "time heals all wounds," it is also true that time perpetuates our wounds, as we are reminded of in the Faulknerian imperative that "the past is never dead; it isn't even past." As we see in these essays, and in our own stories and experiences, the legacy of race and racism still informs so much of our identity, and our relationship to historical memory is a complicated one. How then, to "go beyond the historical, instrumental hypothesis," as Fanon is determined to do, to refuse to "be sealed away in the materialized Tower of the Past"? As with the use of story circles in communities throughout Mississippi, I can hardly claim to understand what would be *sufficient* to achieve this "cycle of freedom"— in Fanon's case, in yours, in my own even. But, as I've seen reflected again and again in the passages of this book, my experience working with communities throughout the state of Mississippi has given me a sense of what may be *necessary* for dismantling the "Tower of the Past": that people move to speak honestly from their own narratives, and can allow other's narratives the justice of human validity. Or, as Fanon puts it: "Superiority? Inferiority? Why not the quite simple attempt to touch the other, to explain the other to myself?"

Oxford, Mississippi 2011

About the Contributors

Lean'tin **Bracks** is chair of the Department of Arts and Languages, and discipline coordinator for the academic area of English at Fisk University in Nashville. She has written *Writings on Black Women of the Diaspora: History Language and Identity* (1997)and the university text *The Black Arts Movement of the 1960's*. She has had work published in *Freedom Facts and First, The Black Scholar, African American National Biography, Encyclopedia of African American Popular Culture, Notable African American Men,* and *Contemporary African-American Novelists.*

Lillie Anne **Brown** is an assistant professor in the Department of English at Florida A&M University. Her work has appeared in the anthology *Black and White Masculinity in the American South, 1800–2000* and in *Southern Quarterly.* She has lectured extensively on the works of Ernest J. Gaines and holds a Ph.D. in American literature from Florida State University.

Ashley **Day** was born in 1971 and has worked for the Southern Poverty Law Center and for the American Civil Liberties Union. She currently lives and works on an organic farm near Tuscaloosa, Alabama.

Foster **Dickson** is a life-long resident of Montgomery, Alabama. He has a B.A. in English and a Master of Liberal Arts degree, both from Auburn University at Montgomery. His career has focused on Southern studies and social justice topics. He is the author of *I Just Make People Up: Ramblings with Clark Walker* and *The Life and Poetry of John Beecher (1904–1980): Advocate of Poetry as a Spoken Art,* and he was the general editor of the curriculum guide, *Treasuring Alabama's Black Belt: Multidisciplinary Approaches to Teaching Place.*

Anne **Estepp** was born and raised in Hyden, Kentucky. She completed her Ph.D. in history at Auburn University. Her dissertation focuses on the Civil War, race, and memory in western Kentucky. She currently teaches at Limestone College in South Carolina.

Jim **Grimsley** teaches writing at Emory University. He has published nine novels, a collection of plays, and a collection of short stories *Jesus is Sending You This Message* (2008). His novels include *Winter Birds* (1997), *Dream Boy* (1997), and *Comfort & Joy* (2003).

Leslie **Haynsworth** was born in Greenville, South Carolina, in 1966, and raised in Columbia, South Carolina, where she still lives today. She holds a Ph.D. in English from the University of Virginia and is co-author with David Toomey of *Amelia Earhart's Daughters*. She is publications editor for the College of Arts & Sciences at the University of South Carolina, where she teaches creative writing.

Ravi **Howard** was born in Montgomery, Alabama in 1974, and he spent part of his childhood in Jackson, Mississippi. His 2007 debut novel, *Like Trees, Walking* is set in Mobile, where Howard currently resides with his wife and son.

Becky **McLaughlin** is an associate professor of English at the University of South Alabama, where she teaches critical theory and film. She has published essays on a wide number of topics including medieval literature, Restoration comedy and modern poetry. She has also published fiction based on her experience in China as an ESL teacher and creative nonfiction based on her childhood in the Mississippi Delta.

David **Molina** has lived in Mississippi since the summer of 2005, when he joined the Mississippi Teacher Corps upon graduating from Amherst College. In 2010 David joined the Center for Writing and Rhetoric at the University of Mississippi, where he ran the Teaching Center. He is pursuing a Ph.D. in rhetoric and public culture at Northwestern University.

Georgene Bess **Montgomery** is an associate professor in the Department of English at Clark Atlanta University. She is at work on two projects: a literary biography of poet, playwright, social activist, and scholar Mari Evans and an anthology of stories told by daughters about their mothers.

Ray **Morton** was born in 1981 and grew up near Birmingham, Alabama. He has a M.A. in history from Auburn University and most recently taught in the social studies department at Booker T. Washington Magnet High School in Montgomery, Alabama. He lives in South Carolina.

Glenis **Redmond** was born in Sumter, South Carolina, on Shaw Air Force Base in 1963, and earned a B.A. in psychology from Erskine College in Due West, South Carolina. She lives in Asheville, North Carolina. She is a 2005 winner of the North Carolina Literary Award and the Denny C. Plattner Award for Outstanding Poetry. She has read on National Public Radio and works as a Kennedy Center Teaching Artist. Her book of poetry *Under the Sun* was published in 2008.

Kathleen **Rooney** currently lives in Chicago where she works as a Senate Aide. Born in West Virginia in 1980, she lived in Shreveport, Louisiana, from 1985 to 1988. A founding editor of Rose Metal Press, she is the author of *Reading with Oprah* (2005), *Something Really Wonderful* (with Elisa Gabbert, 2007), *That Tiny Insane Voluptuousness* (also with Gabbert, 2008) and *Oneiromance (an epithalamion)* (2008).

Dawne **Shand** is working on her first book, a collection of contemporary travel essays about the Black Belt's natural history. Born in 1970, she was raised on her family's farm and attended public schools in Selma, Alabama.

Camika C. **Spencer** is a writer and author of *He Had It Coming*, *Cubicles* and *When All Hell Breaks Loose*. She teaches creative writing in an after-school programs and is an advocate for Arts-in-Education initiatives in urban school systems. She lives in Dallas.

Kyes **Stevens** is a poet from Waverly, Alabama. She was born in 1972 and is the founder and director of the Alabama Prison Arts + Education Project. Kyes and her partner believe in growing their own food and that there is nothing much finer than canned tomatoes in the winter time.

Vallie Lynn **Watson** received her Ph.D. from the Center for Writers and teaches creative writing at Southeast Missouri State University. Her manuscript "A River So Long" was first runner up in the 2009 Miami University Press Novella Contest. Excerpts from the work appear or are forthcoming in dozens of literary magazines such as *PANK*, *Nano Fiction*, *Pindeldyboz*, *Staccato Microfiction*, *Ghoti*, *Metazen*, and *Moon Milk Review*.

Stephanie Powell **Watts** was born in 1970 in Lenoir, North Carolina. She is an assistant professor of creative writing and African American literature at Lehigh University in Bethlehem, Pennsylvania. Her work has appeared in the 2008 Pushcart Prize anthology, *New Stories from the South 2007*, *The Oxford American*, *Tampa Review*, *New Letters* and *Tartts IV: Incisive Writing by Emerging Writers*.

Jacqueline F. **Wheelock** is a retired high school and college English teacher, who was born and reared on the Mississippi Gulf Coast. In 2000, she won the Zora Neale Hurston–Bessie Head Fiction Award for a short story entitled "The Chifforobe." Her stories have appeared in several collections including *Christmas Stories From Mississippi* (2001), and *Christmas Stories from the South's Best Writers*, (2008). She and her husband Donald reside in Madison, Mississippi.

Index